Vicki Lansky

Getting Your Child To Sleep
....and Back To Sleep

Tips for Parents of Infants, Toddlers and Preschoolers

Revised and Updated, 3rd edition

illustrations by Chris Wold Dyrud

Book Peddlers
Minnetonka, MN
book trade distribution: PGW

Thanks to-

Editors:: Kathryn Ring, Sandra L. Whelan and Julie Surma, Judy Berry, &
    Abby Rabinovitz

Consultants:
Meg Zweiback, P.H.N., M.P.H.
Juanita Desmarais, Booth Maternity Center, Philadelphia, PA
Michael Thorpy, M.D., Montefiore Medical Center, Sleep-Wake
    Disorders Center
Gail Farber, M.D.
Michael Meyerhoff, Ed.D.

Cover art and design: Pettit Network   Designer: Alyn Shannon
Illustrator: Chris Wold Dyrud

Special thanks to the parents who shared their words and feelings. Their quotes are reprinted with
permission from Vicki Lansky's Practical Parenting ™ newsletter (1979-1988).

GETTING YOUR CHILD TO SLEEP...AND BACK TO SLEEP
A Bantam Book / July 1985 (Getting Your Baby to Sleep...and Back to Sleep)
Book Peddlers / May 1991, 2nd edition
February 2004, 3rd edition

ISBN 1-931863-05-9

For information on quantity discounts, contact:
Book Peddlers 15245 Minnetonka Blvd. Minnetonka, MN 55345
952-912-0036 • fax: 952-912-0105 • www.bookpeddlers.com

vlansky@bookpeddlers.com

printed in China

04 05 06 07 08 09 10 — 7 6 5 4 3 2

Table of Contents

DEDICATION

To my son, Douglas Dylan Lansky, born May 31, 1970

who, despite giving me years of sleepless nights, grew up to be a wonderful, happy, handsome young man who, as a teenager, slept like a baby—and often did—until noon! Now with a family of his own, he again has sleepless nights to deal with—and I don't!

introduction

When I was pregnant with my first child, the question I always asked of any young mother I met was, "When did your baby start sleeping through the night?" The answer was always…"after a few weeks," or "after a few months." Not so bad, I thought. I could handle that.

It was only later—much later—after struggling to survive with my wonderful (albeit wakeful!) baby boy that I learned that lack of sleep was synonymous with motherhood and that, yes, I could survive a whole night without sleep and live to laugh about it.

Once I made peace with the fact that sleep as I had known it was no longer to be part of my life, I was somehow okay. I stopped being angry about being tired; after that I was only tired. Once I stopped expecting a night of uninterrupted sleep, it didn't bother me not to experience it. Life actually seemed easier.

As that baby grew, I found myself mentally documenting the reasons he woke at night. These included:

- The need for food, attention, or a clean diaper.
- The loss of a pacifier despite the fact that several were strewn about in the crib.
- Those landmarks of babyhood: teething, standing without the ability to sit down, separation anxiety.
- The pain from a string in the foot of a sleeper wound around a toe—only discovered when dressing him to make a trip to the emergency room!

- Illnesses.
- Nightmares.
- Learning to find the toilet during the night.
- And often, no reason I could figure out.

As my son grew and matured, wakefulness at night slowly diminished, but even then there were those nights. One night he called out to me, which was unusual because by then he usually came to my bed. I went to his room and found him stuck to his pillowcase because the gum he had in his mouth when he went to bed (unbeknownst to me) had fallen out of his mouth and had "attached" his face to his pillowcase. We changed pillowcases, bandaged his face to prevent him from "resticking" until we could deal with his skin in the morning, and I climbed back into my bed. That time I had trouble falling back to sleep from the silliness of it all.

But getting a child to sleep-and-back-to-sleep is not the impossible dream.

While there are no real guarantees, there are routines, products, tips, ideas, and approaches that can help you, and they're all outlined here. This is the best of what has worked for parents and child caregivers. It worked for them, and it can work for you, too.

Vicki Lansky

Chapter 1

What Sleep Patterns Can I Expect from My Newborn for the First Six Months?

Sleep. A beautiful word, much on the minds of new parents because getting their infants to sleep is second only in importance to satisfying their needs for nourishment.

If this is your first child, the thrill of being the parent of a wonderful new human being will probably carry you through some sleepless nights, but when you're on duty 24 hours a day, 168 hours a week, the inevitable result is fatigue.

You may feel as if you are living through a month or more of wakefulness broken only by brief periods of sleep. That first month is definitely a long day's night.

Try to relax. Grab sleep for yourself whenever you can (which means when your baby does). Trust your own good judgment, and call on your doctor or pediatric nurse practitioner for advice if you think your baby has any real problems.

And remember two things:

1. You can't spoil a newborn by picking him or her up for nour-ishment or comfort just as long as you think it's necessary.

2. You will look back on these early sleepless days and wonder at how quickly they passed. (Really, you will.)

Infant Sleep Patterns

Your infant's sleep pattern will be as unique as your child is. You cannot control your baby's sleep cycles. Neither can your baby, for that matter. Sleep is not a skill to be learned. Don't let your mother or grandmother try to convince you otherwise! There is no "right" way for a baby to develop a sleep pattern.

During the first six months or so, sleep patterns are often the reflection of your baby's individual biological development. Babies of this age cannot willfully resist sleeping when they are tired, nor can they continue to sleep when they are hungry.

Babies' sleep patterns differ from those of adults in both quality and quantity of sleep. Your baby will have "active" sleep periods (with REM—rapid eye movement), and "quiet" sleep, which is a much deeper sleep, without eye or body movements. During the periods of light or "active" sleep, a baby is easily awakened.

Approximately 50% of a newborn's sleep is spent in each of these states, while an adult typically spends 80% of sleep time in quiet, deep sleep. A baby makes frequent transitions between active and deep sleep and will often wake up during these transitions. This is why your baby will often waken as you are tiptoeing out of the nursery. Rocking and nursing help a baby enter the deeper "quiet" sleep phase.

Babies' sleep patterns also reflect their temperaments. "Easy" babies spend longer periods in deep, quiet sleep and often don't cry when they wake briefly during transitional periods. More "difficult" or active babies carry their waking personalities into sleep, spending more time in the REM periods and waking easily. As your baby matures the ability to pass through periods of light sleep will occur more quickly. However, each child reaches this point at his or her own pace.

A baby will get all the sleep needed provided your baby is not in pain, left hungry, or constantly interrupted. If your baby sleeps very little there is not much you can do except adjust your attitude. Your baby will not suffer from the lack of sleep, but you may. There is also no relationship between health and how much sleep your baby gets. Healthy babies don't have to be good sleepers.

Try not to equate sleep with happiness (yours or the baby's) or superiority (yours or the baby's). Whether or not your baby is a good sleeper, it is not a reflection of your parenting skills or of the baby's "goodness."

How Much Does a Newborn Sleep?

The following sleep patterns are averages only, and it's important to remember that even the experts come up with different averages.

- Newborns usually have about 8 sleep periods a day of varying lengths often just in snatches. Some will sleep from feeding to feeding; others will not.

- Infants' sleep needs vary from 11 to 21-1/2 hours in a 24-hour period.

- It's typical for a newborn to sleep for only 2 to 4 hours at a time. (That means some sleep less and some sleep more.)

Letting your baby determine needed sleep times will contribute to a more relaxed household during these early weeks. When you must alter your newborn's schedule, do so by waking your baby rather than by delaying a feeding.

Infants don't just eat and sleep. Often they are simply awake. So don't expect your baby to be asleep when not being fed. By the second month, a baby may fall into a routine of two longer daytime sleeps or naps, and life will begin to take on the regularity (of sorts) you've wished for.

The transition into a daytime napping schedule versus a round-the-clock sleeping/wakeful schedule happens on its own. It can be encouraged by putting your baby down between 8 and 10 am and 1 or 2 pm. A baby might catnap, have one time of the day that develops into the main nap, or might take two longer, regular naps early on. Many parents choose to regulate their schedules to be home for the baby's nap but, as you can see, if you have a baby who takes long naps, it will inhibit your own out-and-about time. Usually it takes a second child for parents to feel comfortable letting the baby catch shuteye in transit.

Still, with a baby who naps regularly, even if the naptimes are not as long as you wish, life takes on a new normalcy that helps everyone settle down. The transition to the single afternoon nap, sometime during the second year, will be another disruptive period of several weeks' duration that will again require flexibility on your part.

I thought babies slept all the time. Surprise! Surprise!

Joy Goldwasser, St. Louis, MO

Helping Your Baby Get to Sleep

It's much easier for babies to wake up than it is for them to get to sleep. One study found that, on the average, a 2-month-old might need twenty-seven minutes to drop off. The rare "easy" baby may just lie quietly and look around before dropping off to sleep. Others need calming because they aren't able to do this for themselves. These babies can't seem to stop crying, and they get fussier as they become more tired. If you have a fussy baby, time and experience will show you the best way to get your child to sleep.

Set the Stage

- Don't be surprised if your baby falls asleep during or just after a feeding. This pattern will change as he or she becomes more awake and aware. If you feed your baby on demand, you'll probably find that he or she takes more at some feedings than at others and that feeding is a good way to settle down and drift off to sleep.

- When you bathe your baby, make it a warm bath, and then massage his or her body gently, using lotion or vegetable oil you've warmed in the bath water. Plan bath time close to sleep time unless your baby is overtired or has yet to find the bath relaxing and fun.

- Provide a period of quiet cuddling after a feeding. This is the perfect time for a soft lullaby, not for stimulation. Be especially careful to keep things low key. If you have a premature baby who spent some time in an incubator, such babies are often "skin sensitive" as they are generally less mature neuro-developmentally.

- Take your baby outdoors for a few minutes before sleep time to induce drowsiness. A ride in a carriage or a drive in a car often does the trick.

- Let your baby (after a few weeks) sleep outside in the fresh air, if it is not extremely hot or cold. As long as your child is dressed adequately, it seems to aid sleep. In the summer, avoid direct sunlight and protect against bugs with mosquito netting.

- Disconnect the phone or turn the answering machine on while your baby is sleeping.

> When our son was about 4 months old, we put him outside for a nap whenever the sun was shining and the wind was not too strong. He slept well and never caught a cold all winter.
>
> Evelyn Wisniewski, New Egypt, NJ

Strange as It May Sound

- Don't try to keep the house completely quiet. The baby will become accustomed to routine household noises. In fact, some babies can't sleep if it's too quiet. And don't worry about light either, unless your baby is confusing days and nights. (See page 12.)

- Picking up a sleepy, crying baby may wake that child unnecessarily. Calming efforts such as bed rocking or backstroking should be tried first. Some babies, if left alone to cry for a few minutes, can get themselves back to sleep.

- Consider putting a small amount of the perfume you normally wear on the baby's sheet as a comforting reminder of you. Some mothers are careful to use this perfume when they're with their babies in the hospital to start this conditioning. (This may be unwise if your family has a history of allergies.)

- Or put one of your T-shirts or a nightgown into the crib so your scent will be there. Secure the garment so your child cannot become entangled in it.

Snoring is common in infancy. 15% of babies snore in their first 4 weeks of life.

TAKING THE RIGHT POSITION...
WHEN LYING DOWN

In 1997 the American Academy of Pediatrics recommended that babies be positioned on their back or side when being put down to sleep to lessen the possibility of Sudden Infant Death Syndrome (SIDS). Babies must be put to sleep on their backs every night and every naptime by every caregiver. Research has demonstrated that there is a correlation between infants sleeping on their stomachs and SIDS.

If your infant is premature and has respiratory or reflux problems, this may not be advisable but you should consult with your doctor first.

Constant worrying about SIDS, however, and constant checking on a baby, will not safeguard your child from SIDS.

SIDS is <u>not</u>: sleep apnea (breathing stops); predictable; caused by immunizations; caused by colds or neglected illnesses; by suffocation; heredity; or by bad/poor/or stupid parents.

For more information log onto www.aap.org/new/sids/reduceth.htm.

Finding a Comfortable Sleep Position

Vary positions for a newborn. While the head is still soft, it may flatten a bit on one side if the baby is always in the same position. If your baby's preferred position is absolute and you've noticed some flattening, don't be alarmed. Before the skull bones fuse, your baby will be mobile and able to roll over and find new sleeping positions. Encourage the stomach position for playtime. It will also increase back muscle strength.

- Help your baby feel secure by being placed in a corner of the crib or bassinet, with the head touching the crib bumper or a rolled-up blanket.

- You can vary which end of the crib or bassinet you place your baby's head to encourage head turning.

- Put your baby down on a small soft blanket, the same one every night, setting the stage for later "security blanket" comfort. Buy two of one kind to avoid the trauma of separation when one of them needs to be laundered. A cloth diaper can make a good, interchangeable "comfy."

- Help an infant who prefers sleeping on his or her side from rolling onto the stomach position by using a wedge cradle you can buy or tucking a rolled up blanket on both sides of the baby.

The Case Against Using Lambskins for Infants
by a Canadian Juvenile Product Retailer & Mother

Many of you wanted to know why we stopped recommending lambskins for infants. In July 1999 Health Canada, the Canadian Pediatric Society, the Canadian Foundation for the Study of Infant Deaths, and the Canadian Institute of Child Health, made a joint statement "Reducing the Risk of Sudden Infant Death Syndrome" (SIDS), warns parents not to use soft bedding such as lambskins for babies under one year of age. In March of 2000, the U.S.A. Consumer Product Safety Commission, and the U.S. Juvenile Products Manufacturers Association, issued the same warning. The concern is about baby re-breathing air.

When we got the statement from Health Canada, I did not want to accept their advice, since our customers liked using the lambskins so much. But in addition to Health Canada's concern about re-breathing, I also came across an article in Compleat Mother magazine about crib death. Dr. Jim Sprott, OBE, MSC, PhD, FNZIC explained that poisonous gases are emitted from crib mattresses and also from lambskins. Dr. Sprott is from New Zealand which once had the highest SIDS rate in the world and where babies commonly sleep on lambskins. His research shows that lambskins contain the elements arsenic, phosphorus, and antimony, all of which give off poisonous gases.

Some people from the SIDS organization disagree that toxic gases from mattresses and lambskins could be causing SIDS. It is indeed possible that other factors also affect baby's immune system so that a baby is more susceptible to toxic gases. However, the recent deaths of twins lends credence to Dr. Sprott's research. Sadly, the two month old twin girls died of SIDS on the same mattress in a shared crib, within an hour of each other. They were healthy babies.

After about 40 hours of research, I became very certain that Health Canada and the other organizations, and Dr. Sprott had very good reasons for their advice to avoid lambskins. However, the various experts cannot unanimously agree on the cause of SIDS. While the debate goes on, the best thing for parents to do, is to avoid all known risks. Every baby is precious. We don't sell any products which I would not use with my own children.

Grace Marcenkoski (Company President & Mother of 4)

Kidalog/Baby Love/Canada

The LONG Sleeping Baby

While we are pleased when we have infants that can put in long sleep periods, some are questioning the value of this. Some research indicates that nursing babies who sleep in the family bed (discussed on page 82) nurse twice as often during the night as do crib-sleeping nursing babies and take in three times the amount of liquid. Sleeping away from parents (especially for babies who are allowed to "cry it out") may bring longer sleep periods, but this may also cause some dehydration, making the baby more vulnerable to illness and possibly SIDS. It also reduces the amount of touching and holding, a critical factor in infant health. Encouraging lengthy, undisturbed sleep may not be the best thing after all. This should certainly be a welcome note to parents whose babies seem to sleep not at all.

Days and Nights Reversed!

I had a C-section and swore my baby had trouble sleeping at night because we were in the hospital seven days. The lights in the nursery were so bright. So, when we had our second child, I started rooming-in the second night.

Kathie Blanchard, Englewood, CO

There is no night and day in the hospital nursery—glaring lights twenty-four hours a day, babies crying at all hours, people fussing around, PA systems, and machinery noises. Our problem was getting the babies to sleep during quiet times. We had to put them in a noisy room to get them to sleep.

Jeri Oyama, Northridge, CA

On the advice of our pediatrician, we decided on a bedtime (7 pm). Any night feedings were done as quietly as possible and with no diaper changes. I left the lights off and wouldn't take him out of his room or talk or play during feeding. Immediately after feeding, I would replace him in the crib. He fussed some, then started to amuse himself. After about two weeks, there were no more problems.

Pam Smythe, Lake City, FL

I never experienced the reversal because I followed my pediatrician's advice: Do not let the baby sleep longer than 5 hours during daylight.

Carmen Rupprecht, Sanborn, MN

Confusing Day and Night

An infant does not know that night is for sleeping. Only you do. Theodor Hellebrugge, a German researcher who examined the sleeping and waking habits of hundreds of babies, concluded that newborns do not have the day/night body cycles that adults have and are actually more likely to reverse the cycles. So it is up to you to help if your infant is slow to distinguish between day and night.

- Expose the baby to light and dark cycles; trying to implant the idea that when it's dark, we sleep, and when it's light, we're awake most of the time. Keep the baby's room dim for nighttime feedings and changes.

- Put your baby into the regular nighttime crib or sleep place only when it is dark. During the day use a playpen, carriage, or the like in well-lit areas.

- In addition to maintaining darkness at night, also encourage quiet. Don't turn on the radio or TV unless it's "white noise." Keep it dull.

I learned this trick from my sister. When possible I put my infant to sleep during the day in her bouncy seat or in the bassinet in the living room. I only put her in her crib in the bedroom at night so that spot was associated with nighttime sleep. By 10 weeks she was sleeping through the night.

Judy Berry, Plymouth, MN

- Dress your baby in a loose gown to make nighttime diaper changes easier. Use fitted sleepers during the day when you are not particularly concerned if your baby is more stimulated by diaper changes.

- Don't change a diaper at night unless your baby has had a bowel movement or has saturated a diaper and /or clothes.

- Gently "pare off" the ends of daytime naps, waking the baby for feedings during the day and feeding frequently.

- See that even a newborn has some diversion during the day, with plenty of attention and love and the stimulation of music, talk, bright colors, and interesting toys.

- Wake the baby for daytime visitors, in spite of your natural inclination to let sleeping babies sleep! The excitement of having a house full of visitors might be just the stimulation needed to keep your baby awake.

- When you put the baby to bed for the night, try to follow the same pattern every night. Turn off the light, sing a lullaby, or turn on a musical mobile. Whatever pattern you choose, stick to it so the baby gets the message that this is bedtime.

- Remember that this common problem doesn't last very long.

Safety Measures

- Use bumper pads with at least six ties to keep them in place. Remove them (and any stuffed toys that can be climbed on) when your baby starts to stand up, at which time you should lower the crib mattress to its lowest setting.

- Don't leave any teethers or rattles in the crib that could become wedged in a baby's mouth.

- Never use plastic dry cleaning bags to protect a mattress. They are a suffocation hazard if a child becomes entangled with them.

- Don't tie toys across the crib. Suspend them on strings or hang a mobile from the crib bars after infancy. Remove them before your child can stand (around 5 months) as they can become choking and/or strangulation hazards.

- Don't place a baby in an adult waterbed. Babies placed on their stomachs (which should not happen to begin with) cannot necessarily move their heads from side to side to breath. More often the problem is they become entrapped between the mattress bag and the frame.

Checking Quietly....Without Waking

- Leave the door to the nursery open slightly so you don't take the chance of a squeaking hinge or clicking latch waking up the baby.

- Apply WD-40 or petroleum jelly to crib side rails to prevent squeaking when they are raised and lowered.

- Allow enough light into the baby's room so you don't need to turn on an overhead light or a bright lamp. Leave the hall light on or keep a soft night light on in the room. Or install a dimmer switch.

- Be sure your hand is warm when you touch the baby to check for comfort. If your baby's neck is warm, he or she is probably comfortable. If it's damp, your baby's too warm. Warm, pink arms and legs also indicate comfort, but hands and feet usually are cool to the touch.

- Cover the crib sheet with a flannelized rubber lap pad or a soft towel so you won't have to change the whole bed when the baby wets, soils, or spits up on the linens. Rolls of flannelized rubber are sometimes available in fabric stores. They're considerably less expensive than precut pads and you can have the size that best fits your needs.

- Keeping a flashlight near your bed may work for your convenience and safety during the night if your rooms are very dark.

    Avoid the temptation to be available to your child instantly. Babies make noises when they sleep. They may wake and cry just briefly. Sometimes keeping the infant out of your bedroom or shutting the door to theirs will help you overcome the temptation to respond when it is not necessary.

The Light Sleeper

An infant who has been allowed to
sleep only in very quiet surroundings
may indeed become a light sleeper. It
may be necessary to:

- Use a "white" noise, which is
  repetitive and meaningless.

- Minimize wetness and the need
  for diaper changes by double
  diapering. And you don't HAVE to
  change the diaper after each
  feeding if the diaper is only wet.

- Reduce any stimuli that can
  cause waking.

Using a bassinet with wheels allows you to move a sleeping
baby from your bedroom into a hall area, allowing you and your spouse
to talk without waking your infant.

As your baby gets older and sleep patterns mature, this normally subsides. A child over the age of a year who is napping twice a
day but seems to be sensitive to noises may not need so much nap time.
It's important for a child to be sufficiently tired at bedtime.

Listening In

Room intercoms are wonderful items for parents of newborns. They allow you to listen in on your baby without constantly checking the room. They are usually voice-activated. That means the system is silent but turns itself on when the baby cries.

Intercoms usually come in two parts. There is a transmitter, which you place near your sleeping baby, and a receiver, which you place wherever it's convenient for you. One or two parts need to be plugged into an electrical outlet. They need no special installation. Some have receivers that also work on batteries, if you wish to carry the receiver with you. One variety is a single unit that uses your radio as a receiver.

Intercoms are also good for traveling. They can be used in hotel rooms as well as at relatives' and friends' homes. They can also let you know if an older sibling is "checking" on the baby when you feel it is inappropriate or even unsafe.

If you're waking up all night—every time the baby whimpers— it may help to turn the intercom down. Most babies snort, moan, cough and whimper even when they aren't fully awake and need attention. And if you hear your little one crying, wait at least 5 minutes (10 minutes the 2nd night) to give your baby a chance to fall back to sleep by him or herself.

Check with your local retail electronics store, baby mail order catalogs, baby specialty stores or on the Internet for styles and prices.

Causes for Wakefulness with New Babies

During the first month or six weeks of your baby's life, sleeping problems are more likely to be caused by hunger or digestive problems than anything else. Urination may cause a baby to wake until he or she gets used to getting wet (and in two or three years, at toilet training time, this may happen again). Illness and the pain of diaper rash also can contribute to wakefulness.

Hunger and Its Aftermath

Considering the fact that newborns double their birth weight in the first six months of their lives, it's easy to understand why they eat frequently and why their stomachs are stretched pretty tight after feedings. Their gastrointestinal tracts may be under stress. Babies' hunger schedules are individual.

Remember that child-care books offer only guidelines; they didn't have your child in mind as the prototype. And while breast-feeding has many advantages, even that cannot guarantee freedom from digestive problems or colic.

- Be sure your baby is full and well burped before being put down, especially after the last evening feeding.

- Remember that putting more food into an already full stomach) if you're using food as a fast solution to stop crying) can add to a baby's discomfort.

- Stop giving your wakeful or restless baby synthetically colored and/ or flavored vitamin drops to see whether or not this makes a difference. They may cause the problem.

- Breast milk is digested faster than formula, so it might take a breast-fed baby longer to begin sleeping through the night, and the times between feedings may be shorter. Breast-fed babies wake at night more frequently than formula-fed infants. Breast milk forms soft curds in the stomach and is digested rapidly. Formula forms tougher, larger curds that take longer to digest, so the baby feels "full" longer.

Sleeping Through a Feeding?

It is common for babies to fall asleep while nursing or drinking from a bottle when they are very young. This is the sign of a contented baby. Let your baby sleep. If your baby is a bit lazy about "getting through a meal" or your doctor has shown some concern about your baby's growth pattern, you may need to give your infant a little encouragement.

- Try to keep your baby awake through an entire feeding. Jiggle gently and stop occasionally to burp baby. If your baby falls asleep during a feeding and doesn't get enough to eat, your child will soon awaken from hunger.

- Unwrap your baby down to a T-shirt and diaper.

- Wake up a dozing baby while breast-feeding by stopping to change a diaper before offering the other breast.

- Keep some up-beat music on.

- Encourage stimulation from the presence of other family members though some babies will sleep even when over stimulated.

- Sit your baby upright to help with wakefulness.

Allergies and Intolerances

A bottle-fed baby who sleeps poorly and fusses a lot between feedings may be suffering discomfort or real pain because of lactose intolerance—the inability of the digestive system to handle milk sugars—or an actual allergy to cow's milk in the formula. Lactose intolerance can produce stomach pain, excessive gas, and diarrhea. Allergies can cause diarrhea, colic, wheezing, asthma, bronchitis, inner-ear infection, a runny nose or hives. If your baby is having problems, ask your doctor about a formula change. The most common substitute today is soy formula.

If you're breast-feeding, remember that anything you ingest enters your milk supply, just as it once entered the placenta. If your baby is having problems, try eliminating milk and milk products from your diet, especially if you or your spouse has a history of allergies or milk intolerances. But be aware of the nutritional consequences of this (your doctor may recommend a calcium supplement).

You might try eliminating other problem foods for a while, then, add them back one at a time, several days apart, to isolate the trouble-maker.

Unfortunately, the list of suspects is long. First try:

- Anything with caffeine: Coffee, tea, cola, and chocolate.

- Gas-producing foods such as cabbage, dried beans, and onions.

- Fish (especially shellfish), eggs, and nuts.

- Citrus fruits and juices, including strawberries.

- Corn, wheat, bran, oat bran, and oats.

- Check with your doctor about any drugs or medicines you're taking including alcohol, antibiotics, aspirin, cold tablets, nose drops, cough medicines, cortisone creams (used for nipple preparation), and laxatives or fiber-based medications for constipation such as Metamucil.

Diaper Rash

Diaper rash can start on a baby's sensitive skin even if your baby's diaper is changed often. If it is a source of discomfort it may disrupt your baby's sleep. Some say that using disposable diapers will prevent diaper rash, but many others disagree. Some babies have more sensitive skin than others and are simply more prone to getting diaper rash. No matter how careful parents are, some diaper rash comes with the territory. If you've tired all the remedies in your favorite baby book and diaper rash is still severe enough to wake your baby, consult your doctor.

Illness

Newborns come with much built-in immunity, but these wear off in a few months, and then babies become vulnerable to the variety of common but annoying illnesses that can cause restlessness and interrupted sleep. The common cold may be indicated by a fever.

Those wonders of modern medicine—vaccinations and immunization shots—also can cause short-term discomfort and fever that will disrupt sleep for a night or two.

Babies have difficulty breathing through their mouths, and even a slightly stuffy nose can cause a problem. Nasal congestion seems to cause more difficulty with sleeping than eating.

To Ease Nasal Congestion

- Use a nasal aspirator to remove mucus from a baby's nose.

- Use a humidifier or vaporizer; moist air makes breathing easier. Cold vaporizers are recommended because they don't have dangerous heating elements (though hot ones are safe these days). Be sure to turn it on well before you put the baby to bed, so the room will be ready when the baby is.

- Or hang a wet sheet or towel near a heat source like a radiator or air vent in the room to increase humidity.

- Provide better nasal drainage by raising the crib at the head end: Put books under the two legs or put a folded blanket or a pillow under the head of the mattress.

- Run the shower until the bathroom fills with steam; then take the baby in before you put him or her to bed.

Earaches

Middle-ear pressure is often increased when a child is lying down, so the pain of an ear infection often is more bothersome to a sleeping child. Other indicators of a child who may have an earache are crying when coughing or hiccupping, head shaking, and "pushing" against the pain by burying his or her head in your shoulder.

Ear infections need to be treated by your doctor. The doctor who cannot see you till the next day can still advise you by phone on temporary pain-relief measures. Propping a child up and using pain-relieving medication (acetaminophen) may get you through the night.

Ear infections have now been shown to less likely develop with infants that sleep on their backs.

The Early Riser

One recent study indicated that infants' sleep patterns often seem to be related to their mothers' habits during pregnancy. The unborn infants adjusted their rhythms to the mothers', and early-rising mothers bore early-rising babies.

Treat the waking of an infant at 5 a.m. as a night feeding. Change the diaper, feed the baby and both of you should try to get back to sleep. But, as your baby gets older, and has had enough sleep by 5 or 6 a.m., there's nothing you can do to make him or her sleep more. Still, left alone, hopefully your child will entertain himself for another half hour and you can sleep a bit longer.

Older babies and toddlers are often early wakers and, unfortunately for parents who are slow starters, the children are usually bright-eyed, full of conversation, and raring to go. Or worse, some wake up cross and irritable, and full of impatient demands. Many working and single parents use early mornings as their special time with their children. But parents who like to sleep a bit later than their children often take turns getting up early so at least one of them can rest. Others have developed strategies to hold off early risers:

- First, try the old standby: "shhh, go back to sleep," and leave the room. Sometimes it works!

- Attach a shatterproof crib mirror so the baby has "company" in the morning.

- Draw the curtains or install blackout shades so the morning sunlight won't wake your child. Even a heavy blanket will do. Or put the child's bed in a room that isn't exposed to sunlight in the morning.

- Keep some white noise running, such as a humidifier in your child's room, if an adult's early work schedule creates wakeful noises.

- Set a clock radio to go off when your child is usually awake to provide entertainment.

- Provide a place for yourself to doze in the early hours in your baby's room if your presence will quiet him or her and allow the rest of the family to sleep. Share this job with your spouse.

- Allow your child into your bed if it's possible for all to fall back to sleep and you can get that extra hour of shuteye. Otherwise enjoy your relaxing time together.

- Put a favorite quiet toy at the end of the crib or on the floor near the bed before you go to sleep to (hopefully) occupy your early riser.

For A Little Older Child

- For a slightly older baby, hang a little basket on the outside of the crib, and after he or she is asleep for the night, fill it with an assortment of toys, dolls, and books for early-morning play.

- Let your children know that the day doesn't begin until your alarm clock or radio can be heard. Or teach them where seven or eight o'clock is on their clock, and have them play quietly in their room until then.

- Tell them that if it's dark outside, they have to stay in bed. Let a child know that "Mr. Sun" has to be up before your child can get up or out of bed.

- Or pretend to be asleep. Often after a few minutes of waiting, an older child will leave and find something more interesting to do.

- Help yourself to a morning cup of coffee and stretch out on your child's bedroom floor while he or she plays. Catch up on your sleep at naptime—or even next year!

- Have more than one child! Early risers will often entertain each other.

- Leave dry cereal, a boxed drink, or a piece of fruit (such as a banana) out to feed off morning hunger. Be sure the food is easy for your child to reach.

- Or place easy breakfast fixings out (give instructions the night before) so a child can get his or her own breakfast. Kids love the independence and you'll love the extra sleep.

- Set your TV (and volume control) for Sesame Street, or an acceptable video that a small child can turn on alone. This can work in a family room or even your bedroom.

Keep your sense of perspective and be flexible. This won't last. Before long, early-rising children discover how things work and settle in front of the television, especially on Saturday mornings.

Our 3-year-old wakes at 4 or 5 a.m. and comes into our bed. It's lovely to wake up at 6 or 7 a.m., the whole family together.

Susan Varon, New York, NY

I get up when he does and nap when he naps. I look at the bright side. I get some of my housework out of the way early.

Kathy James, Pasadena, TX

Take your child to a 24-hour grocery store and get your shopping done!

Debbi Kapp, Tucson, AZ

One of my earliest memories is being mercilessly disciplined for getting up before everyone else. Because I know first-hand that children are at the mercy of their own internal clocks, I accept that and JUST GET UP with my daughter.

Linda Hasper, Chula Vista, CA

When Will My Baby Sleep Through the Night?

This has become a very important question to new parents, but the real question is: Why is it so important? Obviously it is not important to your baby, or your baby would sleep through the night. What we are really saying is that we, as parents, want to know when our sleep will no longer be disturbed.

When can you expect a full night's sleep? Never soon enough! With a new baby, sleeping through the night is the exception, not the rule.

Somewhere along the way, you'll probably read or hear that your baby should be sleeping through the night by 1 to 3 months of age. Maybe yours will; maybe not. By the end of the first month most babies are waking up twice a night to eat, but usually they will go back to sleep promptly. Lots of babies don't sleep through the night until they are 6 months old.

Of course, you'll have to define the term for yourself: What, exactly, is "through the night"? One set of parents may say with perfect satisfaction that their baby is sleeping through the night when the infant doesn't get them up between midnight and 5 a.m. Another set won't be satisfied until their baby sleeps from 7 p.m. to 7 a.m.

Some people believe that infants can be "trained" to sleep throughout the night, or at least not to cry, but even they agree that it's not likely to happen until the age of 5 weeks or so, and not always then. Methods prescribed invariably involve letting the baby "cry it out" for varying lengths of time. (See 'Crying It Out: Pros and Cons,' page 50.)

Bear in mind (sorry!) that no matter when your baby starts sleeping through the night, it probably won't last. Many babies go through various periods of waking up at night (but we'll save that discussion for Chapter 5).

By 6 months, most babies (83%) sleep through the night. It's at this time, if not before, that you may be able to begin to adjust a baby's sleep to suit your schedule, holding off or moving up the last evening feeding to make morning wake-up time more convenient for you. Some experts set 12 pounds as the weight at which a baby can be expected to sleep through the night. If your doctor agrees, and your baby is getting an adequate intake of milk and solids during daytime hours, your baby no longer needs a feeding after midnight and before five or six in the morning.

Giving Up the Late-Night Feedings

- Wake your baby for the last evening feeding, if you wish, before you go to bed. This works for some but not for others. Some babies will skip the middle-of-the-night feeding right from the beginning.

- Once you are sure your baby is no longer waking from hunger, gradually reduce bottle feedings by two ounces each week for after-midnight feedings.

- Give your older baby (6 to 8 months of age) a bottle of water instead of formula or breast milk. Water is less "interesting" than milk, and the baby may not bother to wake up for it! Or you can accomplish this also by gradually diluting the formula with increasing amounts of water over a period of several weeks until there is only water in the bottle. (See 'Bottle Mouth Syndrome,' page 72.)

Double Diaper Detail

Excess fluids cause baby and bedding to get soaked. If that doesn't wake up your baby, then the diaper change will. Consider double diapering.

- For the baby wearing cloth diapers, this is a fairly obvious maneuver. Simply add a second cloth diaper for double thickness.

- For the baby wearing a disposable, consider inserting a feminine napkin inside the disposable, or take a second or smaller disposable and remove the plastic outer lining. Use this unlined absorbent shell for a double thickness, or fold it into a long, narrow strip and use it as you would the feminine napkin.

- However, today's ultra-absorbent disposable diapers work well.

Will Cereal Solids Help Your Baby Sleep Through the Night?

This is a long-standing controversy that may never be resolved. In the July 1984 issue of Pediatric News, a Gerber Products spokesperson brought up the disparity between published information ("the virtually unanimous response from academic circles is that the introduction of cereal and prolonged sleep are unrelated") and the views of mothers and pediatricians who believe it helps a baby to sleep through the night.

There is no conclusive evidence that feeding cereal at bedtime will promote sleep. But there is no conclusive evidence that it doesn't work, either.

One thing is clear: the baby will not benefit nutritionally from the cereal. And some experts feel you may be setting your baby up for a food intolerance with this early introduction to solids. A baby's digestive tract is usually not ready for cereal or any solid foods until the age of 4 to 6 months.

Yet other data indicates that about three quarters of all mothers do introduce cereal because they believe that their baby is not satisfied with just breast milk or formula, or that this might encourage sleeping through the night. Even when doctors don't recommend it, grandmothers, neighbors, and friends inevitably offer "it worked for me" stories that encourage new mothers to give cereal.

A pediatrician quoted in Pediatric News said: "My rule of thumb is to introduce it when the baby is taking 5 ounces of formula and still acting hungry. If the mother thinks that it will help, then perhaps it will."

Chapter 2

How Do I Make a Soothing Bedtime Routine For My Baby?

Establishing nightly routines makes bedtime easier and more pleasant for parents and child alike. A routine acts as a comfort and settling habit. Babies develop their own comforting habits—rocking themselves, stroking their hair or something soft—along with those you provide—after the age of 6 months.

Many very young babies fall asleep anywhere and may seem oblivious to their surroundings, but it won't be long before this changes. In fact the older a child gets, the harder it can become to settle a child down in a strange place. It is in your best interest to establish a settling-in routine while your baby is young so it will be in place by the time you really need it.

Most babies like to follow the same routine night after night. In fact, as they grow older, they often won't allow a single variation. The routine becomes an integral part of going to sleep, and there's often a temptation to add one pleasant feature after another. Routines include rocking, singing, listening to lullabies, rubbing or patting the baby, and giving a bottle or nursing. After six months or so you'll be able to incorporate reading into your routine. Turn the pages of large picture books and talk about the pictures quietly, or read aloud an adult favorite of yours. Your baby will enjoy the sound of your voice no matter what you read.

Complete the final steps of unwinding for bedtime in the room which your child sleeps—and will awaken. Remember the key is to put your child down while drowsy but still awake.

The following are lists of ideas and approaches to use in your bedtime routine and also to help get your baby, especially a crying baby, to sleep. Try them after your baby has been fed. Try them all, see which ones work for you, and then follow those consistently. Using different or inconsistent approaches daily may confuse the baby. (For more ideas for the older child, see page 107.) A combination of warmth, touch, sound and motion are the basic calming elements. You must work out which combination will work for you.

Cozy Comfort

- Start off with clean, dry diapers. Some babies are disturbed by wet or soiled diapers—others could care less.

- Change the position of a fussy baby who may simply be bored with life from a single viewpoint. Or find out what position your baby likes best—back or side—though back is best. Many parents notice a major difference after they've figured this out.

- Remember that babies love warmth. Lay your crying infant across your lap, tummy down, on a warm heating pad. You may even wish to warm your baby's sheet with a heating pad. (Remember to take the pad out and check the temperature of the sheet with the back of your hand before you put the baby down.)

- Place a diaper between you and the baby when you walk or rock your baby, which will warm it. Place the diaper in the crib first and put the baby's face on it instead of on the cool crib sheet.

- Keep the baby's room temperature at about 70°F if you can. Don't position a crib next to a cold window, a hot radiator or a vent.

- Provide a warm bath as your last activity before what you hope will be the long sleep through the night.

- Keep booties on the baby twenty-four hours a day. Some parents even put mittens on the baby to keep little hands warm.

- Or dress the baby in a sleep sack or sleeper outfit that will cover all over evenly without your needing a blanket.

- Warm a toddler's pajamas for a moment in the dryer on occasion. Be sure any zippers or snaps are not too hot.

Although babies love warmth, overdressing a baby is a common mistake that can interfere with sleep. Normally, little ones need the same amount of clothing and covering as do adults at the same temperature. Check your baby's body temperature by touching the back of the neck, not the hands and feed, which always tend to be cool to the touch.

Physical Calming

- Hold the baby close to your chest and breathe slowly.

- Try holding one of the baby's legs down on a mattress with gentle pressure or crossing arms over the chest and pressing gently.

- Try swaddling the baby—that is wrapping with a blanket so there is constant touch all over the body, and body movement is restricted. Some babies respond better to light swaddling, other to very snug swaddling. Most babies like the feeling of being enclosed. Lay the baby diagonally on a soft receiving blanket, fold up the bottom end and loosely wrap the two sides around him or her.

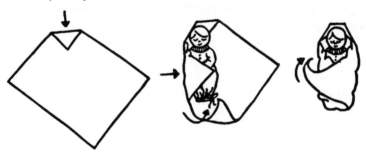

- Knee bends may calm your baby. With your baby on his back on your lap, gently press against the soles of the feet so the knees bend towards the stomach.

- Some babies have an absolute preference for one position when they're held. And it may well be one that is uncomfortable for you. But if you find a position that works, use it!

The Pacifier

The need to suck has been shown to be important to babies even before they're born. This sucking need or instinct serves a baby both as insurance that it will eat and grow and also acts to calm a baby who is neither hungry nor thirsty.

Nursing mothers often come to see themselves as walking pacifiers. Babies often nurse just for the comfort of sucking, and in effect use the breast as a pacifier. Even if your baby has just emptied your breasts, more food isn't necessarily what he or she is after. (The extra sucking helps stimulate your milk supply anyway.) The La Leche League discourages the use of pacifiers, saying that they diminish the baby's urge to suck. But it seems unlikely that anything can truly discourage a baby's need to suck. Not every baby will want or need a pacifier. Some babies have stronger sucking needs than others.

Never hang a pacifier around a baby's neck or
attach it to the crib with a ribbon or string.
Doing so may cause strangulation.

- Satisfy your baby's strong need to suck by giving him or her a pacifier. The safest kind is a one-piece model of molded plastic with a ring and disc too large to lodge in the baby's throat.

- Hold the pacifier in your baby's mouth until your baby gets the hang of it, if necessary.

- Remove the pacifier after your baby has fallen asleep, to limit dependency on it to stay asleep.

- If your baby prefers a bottle nipple, buy one without a hole from the drugstore and let the bottle serve as a holder for the nipple. Never let a baby suck on an "unattached" bottle nipple as it can be aspirated.

- Keep extra pacifiers around—in the crib (two or three in the crib means a better chance of your baby finding one), on your key chain, at Grandma's, etc.

- Use bumper pads in a crib to keep the pacifier from falling out.

- Don't coat a pacifier with sweets (sugar or honey). This adds to tooth decay. It's an "acquired" taste that's unnecessary. A child who likes a pacifier will not need any added inducements.

- Let the baby suck on your knuckle or the end of your little finger. Keep your nail short and turn it down so a hard pull won't force it to scratch the roof of the baby's mouth.

- If you don't like pacifiers, or if your baby won't accept one, help your infant find fingers and thumbs as alternatives—they never get lost or wear out.

- Consider discontinuing pacifier use (if your child lets you) at around 6 months when baby's sucking needs diminish.

- Don't worry about the pacifier habit affecting your child's teeth alignment until after the age of 3. Pacifiers today have been designed with mouth and tooth alignment in mind. Many parents opt to limit the pacifier's use to bedtime and the bedroom, as the child gets older.

Social pressure to limit public use of a pacifier occurs earlier for parents than for children, but ultimately the peer group of each will curtail its use.

Thumbs Up!

Thumb sucking? Ignore it. Sucking is a basic need. Orthodontia is less expensive than psychiatry!

> Betsy Durham, Waterford, CT

Neither of mine sucked their thumbs for more than a few months—I had always thought all babies did—and was ready to accept it.

> Jerri Oyama, Northridge, CA

My child sucked his thumb. My neighbor's four did not. Who needed braces? ALL OF THEM!

> Sharon Herpers, Minnetonka, MN

I used to say, emphatically, that my child wouldn't use one of those things, but when I discovered that my child wouldn't even console herself with her own fingers, I begged her to take a pacifier! No dice.

> Pam Torborg, Armonk, NY

Sound

Your baby loves to hear your voice; it's familiar from all those months in the womb. (Yes, the experts now say that unborn babies can hear what's going on!) Sing to the baby, and don't worry about being in tune. Hum, if your prefer. Or read aloud in a soft, singsong voice.

Read aloud whatever you like. A baby responds to the sound, not the content. Even the sound of your voice from a distance will reassure your child, and can help that child fall back to sleep. Going into your little older child's room, touching or holding him or her may be more disruptive than soothing. Try just talking from the doorway.

- Run a fan, a hair dryer, or the vacuum cleaner for a while. If one sound appears to be more soothing than the others, tape it for a half hour or so, on an endless tape. You can also supply this sort of "white noise" by tuning a radio to a station that's off the air.

- Tape your baby's own cries and play it back to your baby. Some parents find that works like a charm.

- Put a ticking clock in the baby's room. (It works for puppies, why not babies?)

- Play soothing music on the radio or stereo. Or play the piano or a guitar, if you are so inclined.

- Invest in a musical mobile or a music box.

- Turn a water faucet on full force for a baby to watch and listen to.

- Simulate the intrauterine sounds the baby is used to by taping a half hour or so of the dishwasher or washing machine running, and play the tape when the baby is crying or trying to get to sleep.

The Magic of Music

Incorporate music—the same music each night—into your child's sleep routine. Find a soothing tape or CD that you enjoy (you'll be listening to it for a long time) and play it softly. Your little one can learn to associate a favorite composition with sleep. You can use this in the middle of the night as a self-soothing device for a child who wakes.

Music, lullabies and soothing New Age music abounds on tapes and CDs. Yes, I'm partial to mine (page 40), but you may prefer to buy yours from bookstores, baby stores, baby catalogs and the like. Some soft stuffed animals even come with a tape playing device inside so you can play your tapes 'incognito'.

The only danger we've heard about tapes is that they sometimes put the parent to sleep before the child.

This is also the time to brush up on the words to your favorite lullabies. If you wish you could remember the lyrics but can't, you should not have to look too far to find them. You can find hardcover books and ones with beautiful art that all offer your favorite lullabies. Ask at your bookstore. Don't overlook your library as a wonderful resource for books and music tapes. With your computer you can search places like Amazon.com which will give you more options than you thought possible.

Motion

- Buy or borrow a rocking chair and rock your baby in it. Be sure to get one with armrests, and be sure the armrests are comfortable and low enough for you.

- Try rocking the baby from side to side instead of back and forth. Some babies prefer this.

- Look for an old-fashioned cradle that rocks. These were obviously designed for a purpose.

- Gently swing the portable baby basket or bassinet the baby lies in.

- Put the baby in a wind-up swing or cradle swing. Get the one that offers the longest running time, because rewinding may startle a near-dozing infant. Use a scarf to keep a small baby from falling forward onto the padded front bar if you have the swing style.

- Bounce your baby gently on a big bed.

- Or hold the baby against your chest, sit on the edge of your bed, and bounce together.

- Attach special crib springs (usually available in infant furniture stores) to the legs of your baby's crib so you can rock him or her to sleep.

- Use your stroller or carriage for an "indoor" stroll.

- Let your baby sleep in a carriage so you can jiggle it while you're sitting down.

- Keep the carriage by your bedside so you can rock your baby back to sleep during the night. A string attached to the carriage will let you do this while laying down.

- Combine warmth, motion, and sound by putting your baby in an infant seat on top of a running clothes dryer. (But don't leave the baby unattended for even a minute!)

- Take your baby for a walk in a carriage or for a ride in the car (using the appropriate car restraint, of course!). Many a baby has been lulled to sleep by that last ditch effort—the car ride.

• Walk or dance with your baby in your arms or in a soft front carrier or sling. Mom and Dad can take turns with this. Even a back-pack can be padded with towels to "support" a baby.

While motion can help get your baby to sleep, stopping or moving your baby to a bed often wakes the baby up. To describe this as frustrating is a kind understatement. It takes some babies longer to move from "active" sleep to "quiet" sleep than our patience allows. For this reason, some parents opt not to bother transferring the baby who has fallen asleep during daytime hours in a front pack carrier, for instance. Babies do learn to get into "quiet" sleep faster as they grow, and yes, this problem, too, will pass. Parents who continue rocking-to-sleep routines after six months or so, often find that they have conditioned their child to depend on them to fall asleep.

Last Resort

• Burp the baby one more time. A gas bubble may be the only thing between a baby and pure comfort.

• Turn the baby over to someone else if possible, even for an hour.

• Turn off the intercom.

- Put the baby to bed, turn up some music to drown out the sound of crying and take a warm shower or lie down for fifteen minutes or so.

If you usually stay in the room until your baby has fallen asleep, one study of more than 100 8- to 12-month-olds indicates that this may contribute to problem sleep patterns. Those babies whose parents were present until they fell asleep woke during the night twice as often as babies whose parents left the room before they drifted off to sleep. The conclusion: babies need to learn how to fall asleep alone so if they wake at night they feel comfortable about getting themselves back to sleep.

One way to help a baby fall asleep is to take advantage of normal drowsy times during the day. Put your baby to bed at these times, leave the room and make going to sleep your baby's task, not yours.

Chapter 3

Why Does My Baby Cry and What Can I Do About It?

Babies cry because they don't have words for what they need.

The act of giving birth does not grant instant wisdom and intuition on adults. Parents do not instinctively know what a crying baby is trying to tell them. Interpretation is a skill that's learned through observation. It's a trial-and-error process, and it may be different with each successive child because each child is unique.

New parents often expect babies to sleep more and cry less than they actually do. A Boston University psychologist taped the sound infants made during twenty-four-hour periods and found that when newborns are awake, they're usually fussing to some extent. Even when they're asleep, they move around a lot and startle easily. When they wake up they often fuss or cry before they go back to sleep.

Babies cry for a variety of reasons (including filling and exercising those new lungs), and their levels of distress vary widely, but crying basically falls into two categories:

1. Crying communicates a need: hunger, boredom, tiredness, or the need to suck or be held.
2. Crying releases tensions that can't otherwise be expressed and actually can help children "organize" themselves into a sleep cycle.

Crying can be a safe and healthy way for a baby or child to release angry or negative feelings. (This is true for adults, too, although it tends to be frowned upon in our society.)

If the sound of your baby's cry is uncomfortable to you, don't feel bad. I suspect it's designed to be that way.

Crying is probably harder on parents than on babies, though it doesn't look that way. The stress of listening and the feeling of helplessness can be unbearable at times. The frustration of it all can lead to anger. But acting on your feelings of anger against your baby is inappropriate. Hitting, yelling at or shaking your baby will never stop him or her from crying. If calming techniques don't work on your baby and your own feelings are getting out of control, it's always better to let your baby cry safely in a crib while you get yourself out of earshot for at least five minutes.

If your baby cries a lot, buy a relaxation tape. Practice with it using the techniques to calm yourself while your baby is crying or when you must remove yourself from your baby when all calming techniques have not worked.

One comfort is that the fussy crying that seems to reach a peak when the baby is about 6 weeks old usually tapers off when the baby is

3 months old. Colic (discussed in the next chapter) is a common cause of crying during this period. Fussy crying often has a routine time of its own, too. Probably the most common time of the day is late afternoon or early evening, around dinner time, when you have your family's needs on your mind. Try to shift gears for now—take care of your fussy baby, rocking, walking, holding him or her. Consider changing your dinner hour or delegating your chores (or the baby) to another pair of hands. A soft front pack carrier will come in handy at this time of day, especially if you haven't mastered the art of cooking with only one hand.

Although crying is a normal part of development, too much crying works against your baby's self-calming abilities. Look for pre-crying signals and soothe your baby before crying starts. You do want to minimize long bouts of sobbing, if possible.

Crying usually diminishes when the baby's gastrointestinal tract has matured and is under less stress than it is during the first weeks of life. As new motor skills develop, rolling over, thumb sucking, and hand-and-foot watching become more interesting and satisfying than fussing. An infant of this age has also learned to recognize Mom's and Dad's face, so their presence in a room is calming.

Crying will also diminish when the baby gets older and learns other ways of expressing his or her needs. Some people feel that the urge to stop the crying immediately is misguided. Babies (and grown-up, too) need to cry and should be encouraged to do so, they say. You can comfort and attend a baby and still let that infant cry at times.

Also realize that your baby's temperament has a lot to do with the need to cry—and there's not a lot you can do about that!

Your baby's crying has nothing to do with the quality of your parenting.
(Read that sentence again.)

Kinds of Crying

Although every baby's cries are different, some crying patterns have been identified. They may not match your baby's exactly, but you might use the descriptions as possibilities.

• A cry of hunger is usually rhythmical. The baby cries, pauses and then cries again. Remember that during growth spurts, babies get very hungry, and you should adjust your baby's diet accordingly.

• A cry of pain is often loud and long, shrill and urgent. It begins suddenly, stops for a time, and then begins again. Sharp cries may signal sharp pain.

• A cry that indicates the baby has a fever and may be coming down with something or reacting to inoculations is whiny and nasal, often a continuous fussing.

• Cries of boredom, exhaustion, unhappiness, or rage vary from infant to infant and situation to situation. They may simply result from a need to let off steam, and often they indicate fatigue.

Crying Patterns

For a calm and placid baby, a minute may be a long time to cry. A vocal, active baby may cry for as long as five to ten minutes before settling down, and a colicky one may cry more often and for a longer time.

Usually crying is not accompanied by tears until a baby is 3 to 4 months old.

Crying During Feedings

When a hungry baby cries during a feeding, it makes you feel very inadequate. Sometimes—not usually—something is physically wrong. Or your baby may sense tension in you or may be bothered by something else.

- Try relaxing the baby for a few minutes before you start a feeding.

- Hold the baby close handling your child slowly and smoothly. Consciously relax the muscles in your arm so you won't transmit tension.

- Try humming. The repetitive sound will vibrate your chest rhythmically and help calm the baby.

- Let your baby suck on a pacifier to calm down and then return to feeding. Even use a pacifier as part of your feeding routine when your baby has finished eating and still needs to suck.

- Check the nipple by inverting the bottle. If the milk drips out very, very slowly, the hole is probably too small and your baby is working too hard for very little food. Enlarge it by inserting a red-hot needle into the hole. (Hold the point of the needle in the flame of a match to heat and sterilize it.) If the milk comes out in a steady flow, the hole is too big, and the baby is getting too much milk to swallow comfortably. Replace the nipple.

- Don't distract a feeding baby by fondling arms or legs or rearranging clothing. Nursing requires concentration until the baby becomes more experienced.

- Don't allow yourself to feel guilty if feeding doesn't calm your baby. Just move on to other methods.

- Breathe slowly and deeply (using the breathing exercises from your childbirth classes) especially if you're breast-feeding to help you stay relaxed.

Help for Breast-feeding Mothers

Unfortunately, breast-feeding mothers with crying babies are too often encouraged to wean their babies to a bottle. La Leche League International offers help and encouragement to breast-feeding mothers. For information about groups in your area, write to the organization at 1400 N. Meachum Road, Schaumberg, IL 60173, or call 1-800-LA-LECHE or refer to their Internet site: www.lalecheleague.org. You can sign up for a free e-newsletter, the LLLine Chronicle, there.

Comforting a Crying Baby

The same calming techniques used for getting your baby to sleep can also be used with a crying baby (see Chapter 2 and p. 58 for the SleepTight® crib attachment device). In addition to feeding a baby, providing sound, motion, and physical security, parents can also:

- Take warm baths with a baby on your tummy or chest.

- Help your baby find his or her fist or fingers to suck on, in addition to a pacifier.

- Give a massage to relax the baby. Books on infant massage are available if you're not sure where to begin.

- Let the baby enjoy an "air bath" for the freedom of movement. (Undressing your baby completely will also remove the possibility of pain from a thread, pin or tag.

- Change positions or even locations, be it from room to room or going for a ride in a carriage or a car.

Picking Up Your Newborn Baby

It doesn't seem fair that babies will cry after you have done everything you can think of—and it's not—but they do!

As a first-time parent, you may find your fatigue compounded by uncertainty and self-doubt. "Am I suppose to pick up the baby every time he or she cries? [yes!!!] Will it spoil my baby if I do?" [no!!!]

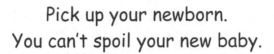

Pick up your newborn.
You can't spoil your new baby.

Don't just pick up your baby when crying. It's important for babies to know they will be held even when not in distress. One study indicated that carrying 4- to 12-week-old infants when they are content or asleep, in addition to carrying them during feeding times or in response to crying, significantly reduces their crying time.

In the first few months you should do whatever it takes to comfort your new baby and help your baby get to sleep. You can always change your baby's patterns or habits after 3 or 4 months.

If you were crying, wouldn't you like to be held?

"Crying It Out": Pros and Cons

Parents' levels or tolerance for crying vary as much as babies' crying does. A crying period of twenty minutes doesn't bother some parents, while to others it's an eternity. Some parents feel that it's cruel to deny love and comfort to a crying baby. They make the point that a crying infant can't be spoiled by being picked up, which is true. Others say that infants who are left to cry it out are apt to suffer later from extreme nighttime anxiety, becoming wakeful and fearful that they've been abandoned.

Dr. Burton White agrees, noting that research indicates that prompt, regular response to crying leads to a better quality of attachment between a baby and his or her caregiver. Another expert says that after about ninety seconds of crying, a baby reaches the point of no return, beyond which he or she can't stop until exhaustion sets in. Of course, a crying baby who's left alone will eventually stop crying, either because that baby doesn't have the strength to continue or because that baby has learned the hard lesson that crying will not bring comfort.

> I would get up when he cried, nurse him, and change him, but no play, He cried, but we hardened ourselves and ignored him. We would set the timer for ten minutes, and he usually was quiet by then.
>
> Becky Gammons, Beaverton, OR
>
> I made sure that he was well fed, had clean diapers, and wasn't too warm or cold. After some soothing (without picking him up), I knew there was nothing else to be done. I just let him cry. Things improved within a few days.
>
> Jeri Wilkes, West Jordan, UT

Some parents take the middle road and respond immediately to a crying baby to find out if anything is wrong and to try to help calm the baby before he or she gets worked up. A new baby shouldn't be expected to "cry it out" if the crying is caused by some discomfort that can be alleviated—hunger, for example, or gas pains that require burping. Once the parent takes care of any problem, or is satisfied that nothing is really wrong, then the baby can be put back down and allowed to cry.

An appropriate response with a crying 6-week-old is not necessarily appropriate for a 6-month-old. A baby over 6 months of age who is still demanding your attention through crying in the night may now be conditioning you. Demands at this age no longer always signal the need for food or comfort, only the wish for it. If your baby's habits haven't changed by this time, perhaps it is time to consider changing yours. In other words, if your baby is 9-,12-, or 16-month-old and not sleeping through the night on a reasonably regular basis and you are exhausted (as distinguished from tired) and you don't like the situation, then you'll have to make some changes. (see "Changing the Deal," page 76.)

Overtired and Over Stimulated

An overtired baby does not necessarily settle down quickly and fall asleep. It's more common for an overtired and over stimulated baby to cry than drift quietly off to sleep. The trick becomes learning to judge your child's fatigue level before it moves into overdrive.

To calm a baby who has passed the point of no return:

- Move into a quiet, low stimulation area.
- Reduce the light in the room, if possible.
- Use motion techniques such as walking or rocking. Rocking may need to be fast and furious.
- Repetitive words or songs or just music might do the trick.

Chapter 4

Is It Colic?

If you have to ask, your baby probably does not have colic. The extended, regular periods of screaming and the very obvious seeming pain of colic are unmistakable.

Colic is not a disease caused by germs, bacteria, or infection, and it's not a sign or a permanent malfunction in your baby's body. It is a symptom of uncomfortable but relatively minor problems. It usually begins when an infant is 2 to 6 weeks old, seems to occur at predictable times, and almost, always ends at about 3 to 5 months with the neurological maturity of the nervous system.

Some experts estimate that 4% to 20% of babies have true colic, although many occasionally display what's known as "colicky behavior." Others claim that as many as 28% of babies have colic. Premature infants often develop colic at 4 to 8 weeks. Colic causes no long term effects on children.

Colic has become a catchall term for any hard, inconsolable crying that can't be linked to a discernible cause. But babies can cry in this fashion without having colic. If you think your baby has it, talk to your doctor, but don't expect miracles. Your doctor may run some tests, but there's really, very little any doctor can do to help. There is no "cure" for colic because it is not a disease.

Colicky babies are healthy, eat well, thrive, and grow.

Defining Colic

You may have heard the terms "evening colic" and "three month colic." They're accurate descriptions; a baby's attacks usually occur from about 6 p.m. to 10 p.m., and colic usually lasts about three months. You may also hear about "grandmother's colic," which nervous parents diagnose when helpful relatives leave and they're left alone with a baby who was "perfect" for a week or so but now has turned into a screaming monster.

Colic Is Not...

It would be most unlikely for your baby to begin to show signs of colic after 2 months of age. At that point, the beginning of colicky behavior probably indicates the presence of allergy or food intolerance. The following symptoms do not in themselves indicate that an infant has colic, but any or all of them may accompany colic:

- Vomiting or spitting up.
- Projectile vomiting.
- Diarrhea or constipation.
- Fever.

- Discomfort during feedings.
- Severe rash, eczema, or other evidence of allergies.

If your baby has any of these symptoms (whether or not colicky behavior is exhibited), have your doctor check for a physical cause. Diagnosis of colic is often done by process of elimination, and it's best to be sure your baby doesn't have some treatable problem before you label it colic.

Colic Is...

Probably the most notable aspects of colic are its severity and its regularity. Your baby will suffer the symptoms and cry inconsolably (rather than the crying suddenly becoming intense) for several hours at a time every day, or almost every day, usually in the afternoon or evening. It gives the appearance of hunger that feeding has not satisfied. The following symptoms are typical of colic:

- The crying is long, loud and furious; often it is outright screaming.
- The baby's face is red, although it may turn pale or bluish after a period of prolonged crying.
- The baby's hands and feet are cold.
- The baby pulls the legs up and appears to be doubled-up in pain from cramping.

- The baby's arms and hands "work" vigorously.
- The baby's abdomen is hard and distended, and his or her back is arched.

Recent research indicates that although babies with colic may grimace, it does not appear to be caused by pain. Colic just seems to be at the high end of the spectrum of normal crying—though it doesn't feel like that to the caregiver.

Your baby's colic is not your fault, and you should not feel guilty about doing what you can to get some relief!

Some Possible Causes

Colic is not caused by your ineptitude. I repeat, colic is not caused by your ineptitude, because so many parents think they are doing something wrong or not doing something right.

Your baby's distress is located within. Although some doctors have claimed colic is related to tension transmitted from the mother to the baby, others (thank goodness) disagree. Any crying, colicky baby can upset anyone within hearing range.

The jury is still out on the causes of colic though every pediatrician has a theory.

Here are some:

- The newborn's gastrointestinal immaturity.

- The baby's central nervous system is immature.

- The baby has a shortage of hormones or digestive enzymes.

- Colic is an allergic response or a lactose intolerance.

- There's a kink or spasm in the baby's intestine.

- Gas is trapped in the baby's intestine.

- The muscles of the baby's colon are overactive.

- A reaction to a yeast infection as indicated by thrush, or sometimes as indicated by a very red and uneven diaper rash.

- The baby is affected by meds the mother took during pregnancy.

There are other digestive abnormalities or structural problems, such as hernial or rectal problems. These conditions are treatable. See your doctor if you suspect either.

Colicky Personality

Some experts have studied the personality traits that seem to character-ize babies who have colic. But it remains unclear whether a particular personality causes colic, or colic causes a particular personality. At any rate, it has been shown that infant personality traits are very often outgrown, so don't live in fear that a colicky baby will grow up to be a difficult child. An extremely active infant may become a calm child, and a tranquil baby may develop into a whirlwind toddler. In a study of children from 4 months to 7 years old, only one fourth of those labeled "difficult" as babies were also considered difficult children. And 61% of the "easy going" babies became more "difficult" as they grew older. According to this theory, a baby with colic:

- Is impatient and irritable.
- Awakens easily and sleeps less soundly and for shorter periods than other babies.
- Shows a general motor restlessness.
- Does not like too much light; cries if a bright overhead light shines in his or her eyes.
- Wants constant physical stimulation…or can't stand any physical stimulation.
- Is as sensitive to sensations from within his or her own body as to outside stimulation.

Relief for Colic

Strategies for relieving colic seem to fall into two categories: those that work and those that don't. There is nothing wrong with doing nothing, because colic is self-limiting and, although it is painful (especially to our ears), it is not really serious and does no physical harm to the baby. But few parents who have suffered along with a colicky baby can imagine doing absolutely nothing. And what works one week may not work the next. It's important to be open to going back and trying ideas that may not have worked before.

SleepTight® Infant Soother

This patented device developed over ten years ago attaches to your crib and simulates the sound and motion of a car ride at 55 miles per hour. It was invented by a desperate parent on his way to the doctor's office. The baby, naturally, finally fell asleep enroute. In one study, 85% of the infants stopped crying within four minutes of using SleepTight®. It has proven to be a successful, noninvasive device to help colicky babies. It's available from $99 and comes with a 21-day money back guarantee. It may qualify under your medical coverage. Call 1-800-NO-COLIC or go on-line at www.colic.com.

Because colicky babies have trouble regulating themselves and the stimuli they receive, parents need to try to help them gain self-control. Usually motion is the first line of relief. It is believed that rocking, for instance, stimulates the inner ear, which helps babies organize stimuli by a sort of "override" that allows them to calm themselves.

A colicky baby makes even the calmest parent feel anxious. Anything you do, any amount of attention you give your baby will not spoil him or her. Try whatever you think might help.

Take advantage of friends, neighbors or relatives. Even an hour off a day can help you cope with the stress of colic. This is especially important if there is an older child. Time off for you and your older child can help minimize sibling jealousy caused by the needed attention paid to the colicky baby.

Network on-line by going to www.colicnet.com.

But Is It Gas?

Not everyone agrees that gas causes much of the discomfort associated with colic. Perhaps it is guilt by association because it often occurs after feedings, legs get drawn up, and gas is released. Since colicky babies don't exhibit poor weight gains, vomiting, or diarrhea, many doctors feel it is not a gastrointestinal problem. Perhaps gas is the result of swallowed air during crying. Still, parents work to eliminate or reduce the possibility of gas as a cause of pain.

Feeding techniques to limit gas pains and cramps:

- Feed the baby slowly and in an upright position.

- Burp the baby several times during a feeding as well as after. Be patient.

- Warm the formula for a bottle-fed baby. Or try cold formula— which may be preferred.

- Talk to your doctor about switching to a different formula.

- Offer warm water after a feeding. It may help "breakup" undigested milk.

- Peppermint seems to have an active ingredient that can help relieve gas. Offer warm, weak peppermint tea. Or even water with just a bit of peppermint flavoring. Let the baby suck on a peppermint candy stick, or dissolve a bit of the candy in a teaspoonful of water. You can also buy a small amount of peppermint spirit from your druggist.

- If you are nursing, give up milk and milk products for the reasons indicated on page 21. Research has shown this to be effective in cases of colicky breast-fed babies. (Colic occurs as often in breast-fed babies as in bottle-fed babies.) You should also eliminate caffeine and foods in the cabbage family to see if that makes a difference.

- Try giving the baby a few drops of a carbonated drink to encourage burping.

- Look into Gripe water. This is a traditional European natural remedy. It usually contains ginger, fennel and some sodium bicarbonate. Gripe water works like a gentle Alka Seltzer for kids. It is available at some health food stores and is also available on the Internet.

- Chamomile tea and fennel tea (weak) are traditional folk medicine remedies. Always cool and dilute herbal teas given to a baby.

Colic Tablets

Some parents report success in soothing babies with a commercial product, Hylands Homeopathic Colic Tablets, which claim to relieve gas pains and the distress associated with colic. These are available in health food stores, from on-line sources or from Standard & Hylands Homeopathic Co., P.O. Box 61067, Los Angeles, CA 90061, 800-624-9659. (www.hyland.com)

The ingredients are natural—wild yam, chamomile, bitter apple and lactose. The tablets are to be dissolved in a teaspoonful of water. Because of the high dilution of these homeopathic tablets, it is safe to try them if you wish. There is no clinical evidence that they are effective in treating colic.

What Got Us Through

A tip from a La Leche League newsletter helped me. Lay your baby astraddle in your arm with your hand holding the crotch, baby's head at your elbow, with head slightly higher than feet. Our daughter usually fell asleep in that position.

Billie Salas, Albuquerque, NM

One thing that made four weeks of colic easier for me to bear was realizing that my child was actually in pain and needed all the love that I had to give.

Brenda Hickman, Forest, VA

We had a prescribed colic medicine that worked wonders at first, but it wore off after a while. Then we went back to the old stand-bys—pacifier, bouncing the baby, tummy rubs, and liquor—for us—not the baby!

Sandy Heath, Brownsville, TX

I don't know who cried more—Mom or the baby. I think being able to get away a little helps, even if it's only for a short walk when Dad gets home. Also talk with other parents. You need to realize that you're not the only one with this problem.

Debbie Ulrich, Lewiston, MN

You never forget your baby's colic. Ours lasted three months and it was dreadful. I will never forget that early morning I had reached my limit. The shrill, nonstop shrieks were piercing. I was about to throw my baby out the window—then I looked down at her, and she gave me a big smile. My heart flip-flopped. That smile helped me endure another month before she finally outgrew it.

Hallie Lerman, Los Angeles, CA

I had three babies that would qualify as colicky, including two at the same time—twins! I'm glad I had been through one colicky baby before their arrival. I know that first experience helped me cope with two babies who cried and could not be comforted for hours at a time every day for several months. What got me through? Remembering it really doesn't last very long (but, believe me, I really do remember that every day with a colicky baby seems like a year!) and knowing that my baby didn't want to cry all the time any more than I wanted him to cry all the time.

Karen Gromada, Cincinnati, OH

A colicky baby affects the whole family, because the time a fussy baby takes (and needs) takes away from others. It might help to hire a teenager each day to help with the other young children. And feel free to cry, go into a room and scream or do whatever you need to do to relieve the tension of not knowing how to help this little person. Try to maintain a sense of humor. (Know any good colic jokes?)

Carol Eggers, Wayzata, MN

Positions to Try for Relief of Gas and Cramps

- Let your baby sleep face down across your knees for a short period. Also, put a heating pad or warm hot-water bottle under your baby's tummy. Be sure it's not too hot and that one or two layers of fabric are between the skin and the heating source. Put a hot-water bottle between your body and the baby's tummy when you walk him or her, too.

- Or try laying the baby on one side for a few minutes, then raise back to an upright position.

- Give the baby a belly massage, gently pressing your fingers in a clockwise direction around the stomach area until gas escapes.

- Sling the baby over your shoulder, with your shoulder pressing into the intestinal area.

- Rest the baby on your hip, facing outward, and let the stomach area drape over your arm.

- Put the baby face up on your lap and push the knees up toward the chest.

And of course, don't forget to try a mechanical swing or vibrating bouncy seat to get relief from colicky crying.

Last Resorts for Relieving Painful Gas

- Insert and remove a small glycerin suppository part way into the baby's rectum.

- Or insert the tip of your little finger or the bulb of a rectal thermometer, lubricated with petroleum jelly. It might help painful gas to escape.

Pros and Cons of Sedatives

Doctors may prescribe medications which fall into two different categories. One is an antispasmodic medication to decrease intestinal irritability. Or, if the doctor feels colic is related to the central nervous system you may be prescribed a mild sedative.

Many doctors feel it's reasonable and practical to prescribe a sedative for a baby with severe colic, as much for the sake of the parents' health and sanity as to the baby's comfort. Some prescribe a drug for only two or three weeks, hoping to break the crying habit, but others suggest it be used as necessary.

As with any other kind of drug (alcohol, for example), side effects are possible. An infant may have a "paradoxical reaction," becoming hyperactive instead of quiet and relaxed. In some cases, the baby will have a "hangover" and be irritable and fussy the next morning. Other babies are not helped by sedatives. Sleep research seems to indicate that most sleep medications do not induce normal sleep so this is truly only a short-term solution.

Apparently, no good studies support the effectiveness of the use of medications.

Some parents are reluctant to sedate an infant and will use a drug only under extreme conditions. Sometimes just having it on hand and knowing they can use it makes them feel better.

Chapter 5

How Do I Coax My Night Waker Back to Sleep?

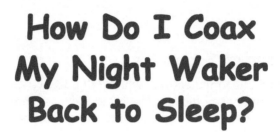

Some babies who have no trouble falling asleep may still wake up several times during the night. Others may sleep through the night for a few months and then go back to night waking for awhile. For many a child, simply waking in a dark room may create a need for your reassurance and the knowledge that you are nearby.

In our culture, it's a rare child who goes to sleep every night at a reasonable hour (translation: convenient for his or her parents) and sleeps straight through for ten to twelve hours. It's said that 95% of all children are night wakers at some time during the first five years of their lives. Night waking frequently occurs when babies develop new developmental skills at around 6- to 12-months.

Babies usually wake more frequently with changing sleep patterns in the second half of the first year. And, discouraging as it may be, only about 50% of all babies sleep through the night at age 2.

But Why Me?

- Babies and children who are busy during the day are often busy at night, too. Some say that the bright, active baby who demands a lot and crawls, walks, and talks early sleeps less than a passive one. Others say it's the thin, wiry baby who sleeps less than the plump one.

- Too much sleep during the day can also keep a baby up at night. If your baby is waking more than once a night, try providing more stimulation during the day to keep him or her awake.

- Developing motor skills may also keep babies from sleeping if they are able to stand up in a crib but are not yet able to get back down, or when they can flip themselves over onto their back but can't get back onto their stomach. While this may be frustrating and tiresome for you, shift your perspective for a moment and realize that it's no picnic for your baby, either. This brand new world is getting exciting and challenging and frustrating. Night waking usually subsides once the new skill is mastered.

- Vacations and breaks in the usual routine will not only cause children to go off sleeping schedules while away from home but also may cause a period of adjustment to their regular pattern when returning home.

- Children from age 1-1/2 to 3 years may be wakeful because of jealousy of a new baby in the house and perhaps a move to a new bed, nightmares or night terrors, and, if toilet training has begun, a wet bed or the fear of wetting it.

- Many children are easily conditioned to awakening at night to enjoy the short-term, solicitous actions of their parents when being attended to for an illness such as an ear infection.

- Some doctors and nutritionists feel that improper diet can also cause wakefulness. They recommend restricting sugar intake and avoiding artificial ingredients (especially food coloring) and caffeine, which a child may get in soft drinks and chocolate.

- By the middle of their first year, babies begin to suffer from what's known as separation anxiety. They worry that when Mommy/Daddy/ primary caregiver goes away, he or she won't come back.

Keeping a child from taking a needed nap as a way to induce sleeping through the night is a poor idea, unless the child is ready to give up naps altogether. Disturbing a child's sleep cycle increases the chances of night waking.

If you know your child no longer needs nighttime nourishment, avoid the temptation of nursing or offering a bottle unless you are prepared to be awakened the next night for more of the same.

You can inadvertently reinforce undesired wakefulness on the part of your child by rocking the child or keeping the child company until sleep comes. We all provide these comforts on occasion. If you find these are not just occasions but nightly occurrences—and usually at the same time each night—then realize you can change your child's behavior only by changing your response to your waking child.

Have You "Trained" Your Child to Wake at Night?

- By responding to every cry with a breast or a bottle, you can accustom your child to small feedings so your child begins insisting on "snacking" through the night.

- By acting the role of the sleep calmer so your child doesn't have to learn this technique for him or herself.

- By providing company for your trained night crier.

To Encourage Weaning
- Let another family member put the baby to bed while you are out of sight.

- Be prepared for a night or two of tears before the adjustment is made.

- Tell your child the bottle is lost or broken. (I can't think of an equivalent excuse for nursing mothers except to let Dad take over the bedtime procedure!)

- Keep your tired toddler up later so that nursing or bottles are forgotten at bedtime.

- Substitute other calming routines such as rocking or back rubbing, or give your child a nipple attached to an empty bottle to suck on.

Bottle Mouth Syndrome

Do not put a baby over the age of 12 months to bed with milk, formula, juice, or any sweet drinks in a bottle. It can (and does) decay your baby's new teeth. Babies need their baby teeth for eating and for correct formation of their mouth. Permanent teeth don't come in for many years. If a bottle is necessary for your bedtime routine, fill it with water only. If your baby is accustomed to a milk bottle, gradually dilute it (1 oz. water to 7 oz. milk, then two days later use 2 oz. water to 6 oz. milk, etc.). In two weeks your baby will be on a water-only bottle. (Use this same technique to wean a large (over 6- to 8-month-old) baby from a middle-of-the-night feeding.

Teething

When your baby is anywhere from 4 to 9 months of age, it is common to start to awaken because of teething pain. This usually lasts a day or two per tooth. The problem is more severe when several teeth come in at once, or in rapid succession.

Babies differ in how they react to teething, some unfortunately having quite a painful time with it. Those children will be fussy and go through crying jags during the day or night. A teething baby can often be distracted from the discomfort during the day by a change of scenery or activity. Nighttime is a bit harder.

- Ask your doctor about using acetaminophen to relieve the pain.

- Check for over-the-counter products, such as Baby Orajel®, that don't contain alcohol.

- Keep an extra pacifier in the refrigerator or freezer. The cold should soothe the pain and the pacifier should soothe the baby.

- Items that can bring relief by chewing on them are: teething rings, a toothbrush, washcloth, or a stale bagel.

> I think the best way to help a child sleep through the night is to not worry about it. I don't know many adults who don't wake up at least once during the night. At one time this meant getting up and playing with him at 3 a.m. Now it rarely means more than a pat on the back.
>
> Gail Nagasako, Hailuku, HI

Midnight Options

For many months parents, in effect, help their babies to sleep by providing calming procedures for them such as rocking or giving them a bottle. So babies become conditioned to parents' intervention. As they mature and their sleep cycles fluctuate between deep and light sleep periods, babies must learn to get themselves back into that deep sleep alone rather than calling upon the parents for help. It becomes the parents' task to "teach" their children to go to sleep on their own.

- Attend to your child with firmness and reassurance but without contact or extravagant attention, to convey the message that it's your child's job to fall back to sleep.

- Sit near your child but avoid touching and eye contact so your presence allows the child to settle himself or herself.

- Some parents have a place to sleep in the child's room it they feel their presence is needed, as in the case of illness.

- Encourage a night-waking child to be independent and play quietly alone in bed. Put several pacifiers in a baby's crib. Put dolls and toys in an older child's bed but only after the child has fallen asleep. Sometimes a night-light is necessary for the child to locate available objects.

- Go to a wakeful child at 15 minute intervals, if necessary, and say in the same words every time that all's well, it's time to sleep now—but without picking up your child.

- Offer reassurances from the doorway where the child can hear but not see you.

- Let an older sibling share the younger child's room (or vice versa) to deal with separation anxiety or loneliness.

- Leave a small bottle of water where a thirsty child can reach it without crying out for parental attention. If you feel you must provide the drink, offer a cup, not a bottle.

- Tell an older child a story about the sandman who occasionally leaves a small surprise gift under the pillow of a child who doesn't wake others in the middle of the night. Be sure to follow through!

My 18-month-old son goes through periods of waking at night. I keep a light on low for him and just pick him up briefly to reassure him. I do not offer a drink because if I do, he'll wake at the same time the next night.

Donna Stelzer, Englewood, OH

My 2-year-old daughter was frequently awakened in the night by heavy wetting, in spite of the extra-absorbent diaper. Now I insert an extra-absorbent feminine napkin (self-adhesive) in the front of the nighttime diaper, Result? Happy parent, dryer child, and more sleep for all.

Melissa Behnke, San Francisco, CA

"Changing the Deal"

Sometimes whatever you are doing is not working. Some parents simply change their expectations. Others "change the deal," especially if they have grown weary from repetitive nighttime wakers. This is often difficult because we as parents have to move away from the notion of gratifying our child's every need—which is the role we play with a newborn. Indeed, often it is the child who is used to parents gratifying every daytime need who also expects every nighttime need for calming to be met by Mommy or Daddy. So we have to work at undoing the job we did so well.

You can begin the process gradually. First wait five or ten minutes, rather than rushing in to calm your child. If you must go in, offer minimal measures: pat or rub the back gently, cover your child, give verbal assurances including words to the effect that it's time to go to sleep and you'll see Mommy or Daddy in the morning. If you need to change a diaper, do so in the bed so as to minimize physical contact. Be consistent and avoid the temptation to feed and hold your child.

For the child who still continues to wake for "wants" rather than "needs," crying it out ultimately is the method you may have to use when all else fails, though not everybody agrees with this concept. Many do believe that if you truly wish for a night of uninterrupted sleep in the near future, you will have to let your child cry. It is reasonable to first make a quick check to be assured that nothing is wrong, but then you must walk out quickly. It seldom takes more than two or three days to reduce nighttime crying episodes, though each of these nights can feel like an eternity. In fact, during this period the crying may get worse before it gets better.

Pediatric nurse practitioner, Meg Zweiback has dealt with

families when letting a child cry it out has not worked. She feels it is better to "bore a child to sleep." Simply visit your child at fifteen minute intervals for reassurance and a pat on the back so your child does not feel deserted. But also do not pick up or feed your child. This method, too, does not work overnight. So give yourself a week for it to take effect.

Only once children are older and more independent can changes be based on consequences and incentives.

Here are some suggestions to get you through when you must "change the deal":

- Make sure that you really want to "change the deal," and it's not just something you're doing at the suggestion of a relative or neighbor.

- Keep a sleep diary for a week, jotting down your child's sleeping times and wakeful habits and your responses as they happen. Tired parents shouldn't rely on memory. This diary can give you accurate information so you can see more clearly what you want and need to change.

- Decide together with your partner on an acceptable plan, and stick to it.

- Pick a time of relative calm in your family life—not the week you start a new job or bring a new baby home.

- Tell your child at bedtime that you are not going to come in at night. This won't prevent the waking (or the crying) but it will begin to establish a verbal link to the desired behavior.

- Use a clock or timer as your indicator for the length of time you will let your child cry, or to clock just how long he or she has been crying. Don't rely on a gut reaction—your gut will be in a knot.

- Do not peek into your child's room or let him or her hear or see you.

- Try to get yourself out of hearing distance.

- Turn up the volume on the TV. It can make crying easier to bear.

- Warn neighbors about your plan if they are within earshot. They will most likely be understanding.

- Hire a babysitter for the night, or time your new plan with a short vacation if you can't handle the crying. It never seems to bother someone else as much as it does the parents.

Serious Sleep Help—For You or Your Child

When nothing seems to work and you know you need more help, you may wish to contact a sleep disorder center near you. Most are now beginning to offer help with pediatric problems. For a free booklet listing centers around the country, contact:

National Sleep Foundation
1522 K Street N.W., suite #500
Washington, DC 20005
202-347-3472
www.sleepfoundation.org

- Give a change of pattern time to work; it won't happen overnight. Four days is realistic. You might have to work this pattern more than once over a six-month period.

- Try again in a few months if this hasn't worked after several days. A few months can give a child more maturity to handle your "new deal."

- Keep in mind that once your child has seemingly "learned" to get back to sleep (or stay asleep), the old behavior often reappears a week or two later. After checking your child to make sure all is well, return to your original plan.

The Word from those Considered 'The Wisest'

Though there are many books by professionals to help you get your child to sleep, three authors stand out whose books are particularly popular with those coping with sleepless babies—Dr. Richard Ferber's "Solve Your Child's Sleep Problems", Tracy Hogg's "Secrets of the Baby Whisperer", and Dr. Marc Weissbluth's "Healthy Sleep Habits-Happy Child" and "Your Fussy Baby". These authors share the principle that sleep—or at least going to sleep—is something a child must learn and must learn to do by oneself. If you do it for a child, you will be doing it for a LONG time as the child will not be able to get to sleep without your help.

Dr. Ferber from the Center for Pediatric Sleep Disorders at Children's Hospital in Boston, is widely recognized as the nation's leading authority. His method, introduced in 1986, offered new parents proactive advice on developing good sleeping patterns and daily schedules to ensure that sleeping problems don't develop in the first place. His book stresses the importance of being consistent. Ferber does not advocate "crying it out" but rather "crying in moderation" to solve sleep problems, though to many his message is that of "crying it out". The goal, he states, is to create correct sleep associations. It is O.K. for children to cry if you have met all their needs. The message should be, "I AM here if you need me, but you DON'T need me". The Ferber technique, we are reminded by those who disagree with his position, does not work for everyone. There are no studies that have examined the long term mental health impact on babies who have been "ferberized".

Tracy Hogg, a neonatal nurse, teacher, and mother of two, uses a little gentler technique. Focusing on newborns and their parents, her simple programs are a blend of intuition and methods based on years of experience. The first half of her book is devoted to E.A.S.Y.— (eat, activity, sleep, your time)—her name for creating a structured daily routine for you and your baby. Techniques for 3 month olds (back patting and shh-ing and swaddling) are different than those for 8 month olds. Wind-down, quiet activity is important as the child gets older. Back patting—which is important—needs to be done in the center of the baby's back. It should not be done timidly and it should also be done in the rhythm of a clock. "Shh-ing" volume needs to be loud. Helping children settle down while maintaining physical or visual contact (using one's voice and hand without picking them up, rocking them or feeding them) may need to be a full 20 minute process, she feels. For more details refer to her book or her website at www.tracyhogg.com.

Dr. Marc Weissbluth, a pediatrician and father of four, has been writing books about crying babies since 1984. He offers encouragement, support and insight along with strategies to help babies sleep so parents can reclaim their lives.

A Midnight Cowboy?

Once your toddler learns to get out of the crib, you face an additional problem: he or she may wander around the house during wakeful periods at night. You should childproof the child's room, and just to be sure, lock all doors and windows in the house as well.

- Install a gate at your child's door if you're worried about nighttime adventures. Or attach a bell to the child's door so you will be awakened if your little one leaves the room.

- Leave on a night-light so the child won't stumble over toys or furniture.

- Supply a stool next to the crib to help the child you know will climb out. You may prevent a bad fall.

- Consider having the child move up to a big bed. This will probably increase the possibility of getting out of bed but it can limit falls.

> Kelly, our 3-year-old, would wake up in the middle of the night wanting to play. Since she loves to read, my husband put a reading lamp on her headboard with a dimmer switch. When she wakes, she turns on the lamp, reads a book or two, turns the light down or off and goes back to sleep.
>
> Freda Russell, Wendell, NC
>
> Our 5-year-old gets one Hershey Kiss in her lunch box if she sleeps all night in her bed the night before.
>
> Saundra Kaplan, Mt. Vernon, NY

Chapter 6

Should We Allow Our Baby in Our Bed?

One way to help everyone in the house get a good night's sleep is simply to take your baby into your bed. Some parents choose this as their regular routine. Others use it only when a child is wakeful, ill or frightened. They either let the child spend the rest of the night in their bed, or they return the child to his or her own bed after the child falls asleep.

This notion still horrifies many parents and will evoke more negative responses than not. Parents who share their bed with their children usually don't volunteer the information, knowing the bias against it. And yet, the United States is one of the few countries that has a cultural bias against the family bed. Families in most other countries sleep together routinely. In Japan, for example, it's very common, and not just because of a lack of space. The cultural emphasis there is on the nurturing aspects of family life.

Over the years this once common tradition fell by the wayside in the United States as childcare experts added extra pressure to the psyche of new parents, warning them that they would create psychological scars for their children if they didn't teach them to sleep by themselves. (Note, however, that parents do not sleep alone. Actually, who does like sleeping alone? Why would a baby?)

The Family Bed

"The Family Bed: An Age Old Concept in Child Rearing" by Tine Thevenin is the original bestseller on co-family sleeping arrangements. Thanks to the impact of this singular book, many of these fears and taboos have been set aside. The book explores the history of the family bed, variations and benefits of co-family sleeping, and gives "permission" to interested parents. It explores the pros and cons, and the joys and irritations that occur when children sleep with their parents. Today, even respected professionals—physicians and child psychologists—have softened their positions—or have even taken up the banner of co-family sleeping.

Weighty Concerns

The concern most parents raise about sleeping with their children, especially with new babies, is that the child will be smothered or crushed. Remember, however, that a baby is not completely helpless or passive. If a parent starts to roll onto the baby, he or she will most certainly wake up, make a noise, and start to cry. A baby will not just lie there and allow itself to be smothered!

A restless baby will take time to adjust to, and a damp bed may never feel right to you. A baby who likes to play at night may change your mind about co-family sleeping. The experience may be more or less pleasant for you depending on the various ages, stages, and sleep patterns of your children. Try to be flexible and open-minded. It doesn't have to be a "now and forever" decision.

> When I advised against bringing children into their parents' bed in an earlier article, I received many letters from parents who felt that "sleeping alone is a custom our society unreasonably demands of its small children." I was impressed and have learned a great deal from the letters that expressed this point of view. I hadn't realized how many parents did NOT believe in helping a child learn to sleep alone at night. Their letters and their arguments made me reevaluate my rather rigid ideas on handling sleep problems in our culture.
>
> T. Berry Brazelton, M.D., Redbook, June 1979

The Sexual Dilemma

Professionals used to discourage families from sleeping together by saying it caused all sorts of sexual problems in children. This now is acknowledged to be more fiction than fact.

Parents who practice co-family sleeping believe that it is likely to reduce (rather than increase) the chances of sexual child abuse occurring because it gives parents a way to fill, in a nonsexual way, their need to touch and be touched. Any parent having this deep-seated, personal problem will find an outlet for this more often in the privacy of a child's own room.

The issue of sexual privacy between husband and wife is seldom a problem, unless one partner wishes to see it as such. As always, it's important to keep the lines of communication open. You and your spouse need to be honest with each other about your own needs and be responsive to the needs of your baby. Be clear about your feelings about co-family sleeping. How long will it last? Can you come up with some compromises that will make it more workable? A study from Sweden indicates that the parents' marital relations were not harmed by having a child sleep with them and that it did not cause a rise in the divorce rate. Take advantage of the baby's longest, deepest period of sleep for lovemaking. Or leave the room quietly and go somewhere else for privacy.

Children over the age of three often like to come into a family bed even if they didn't at younger ages. Nightmares and new anxieties push them to the security of their parents' bed.

Advantages

- It fulfills the natural human need to be with someone. It gives the child a feeling of security and of being loved and protected. Feeling the body heat of another person is very comforting. There is no need to be afraid.

- A baby may fall back to sleep faster if you respond before he or she is fully awake. You are right there if your baby needs something. Your presence helps a baby relax and fall back to sleep.

- Both parents and child may sleep better. There's no need for a parent to jump out of bed and run down the hall when the baby cries or wakes.

- It may create a closer bond between parent and child. This is especially true for fathers, who often see their children for only limited periods of time during the day.

- Many parents feel it cultivates independence by supplying strong early feeling of security.

    Obviously this choice is a personal one. Many parents can't imagine having their children in a family bed; others can't imagine keeping them out.

Family Bed Logistics

- Set the crib mattress at its lowest point, put one crib side down, and pull the crib against the parents' bed. The baby still sleeps in the crib but can be moved freely back and forth. This is an especially good arrangement for a baby who spits up often, making that child an unattractive bed partner.

- Reduce the risk of SIDS. Put your baby to sleep on his or her back. Use a foam wedge between your little one and your spouse to prevent rollovers.

- Or allow the child to sleep between the parents.

- Or push the bed against the wall.

- Or give up the bed altogether and sleep on mattresses, sleeping bags, or air mattresses placed close together on the floor.

- Place your baby between you and a guard rail you've attached to the side of the bed.

- To prevent your own discomfort, in case your baby leaks onto or wets the bed, put a rubberized flannel pad between the sheet and the mattress. Put a towel under the child as a temporary middle-of-the-night solution. Or plan ahead and double-diaper your child.

- Keep quiet toys within easy reach so a restless or early waking child can play without waking the rest of the family.

Variations on the Theme

- If your baby has trouble falling asleep, bring that child to bed and nurse and cuddle until asleep. Then you can either return your baby to their own crib or keep the baby with you for the whole night.

- Let children start out in their own beds, with the understanding that they are welcome in your bed if they feel a need to be with you. This gives the children a feeling of security and the parents a bit more privacy.

- Get into bed with a child old enough for an adult-size bed until that child falls asleep.

- Or let a child fall asleep in your bed with the understanding that your child will be carried to his own bed later when asleep.

- Expect children who are brought up in a family bed to voluntarily stop sleeping with their parents by preschool years. As children get older, they need the security of their parents' presence less. At that time children may begin to prefer sleeping with a sibling instead, either in the same bed or the same room.

It's Not for Everyone

I can never believe it when I hear about people sleeping with their kids! We tried it with our toddler when he woke at night and it was great if you like drool on your pillow and being kicked constantly in the back. His favorite was to say "eye" and stick his finger in your eye. Can people really get any sleep with little kids?

Priss Baker, Aurora, CO

At infant and toddler stages, I can understand it for comforting, but neither my husband nor I encourage it. Our son has been in his own room since he was 3 weeks old and seems none the worse for it. Both parents and children need privacy and spaces of their own.

Patrice Cyron, Long Branch, NJ

We shared a bed with our daughter on a vacation when she was 18 months old. None of us got our proper sleep. When we returned home she could not wait to get into her own bed. And neither could we!

Helen Snelgrove, W. Bloomfield, MI

Alternatives to the Nightly Family Bed

- Let a lonely child sleep on a mattress, couch, futon or sleeping bag on the floor in your room.

- Set certain times when your child may come into your bed. Some families like to wake up together and allow the children to come in early in the morning. Others like weekend-morning family times.

- Use an incentive chart for a child you don't want in your bed: a star for each night in his or her own room, a special treat for a week of stars, etc.

Play it Safe

- Don't combine drinking or using sleep medications when you have a baby in your bed.

- Use a firm mattress. Avoid waterbeds. Check for gaps between the bed frame and mattress as well as the bed and the wall where a baby could get stuck.

Chapter 7

How Do We Cope with the Loss of OUR Sleep?

People who say they "sleep like a baby" usually don't have one. Some days it seems as if your baby never really sleeps at all—retires late, arises very early, and catnaps only occasionally through the long day. Babies always get the sleep they need. The same cannot be said for us. While our sleep deprivation is not a threat to life or health, it certainly affects our sense of well-being and our ability to cope with stress.

It's not fair that just when we need the greatest amount of energy to cope with all the changes and demands a new baby brings, we have the least. But—forgive the repetition—nobody ever said life as a parent was fair. Remember, nursing babies simply wake at night more often in the beginning and require more feedings as breast milk is digested more quickly than formula. Still, it's a worthwhile trade-off. Parenthood is thrilling, challenging, and fun (believe it or not), but it's not always fair. You're probably focusing most of your attention on the baby; that's perfectly natural with newborns. But if you're to maintain your own sanity, you're going to have to think about yourself a little too.

Parents with two or more young children who are night wakers are often understandably fatigued. Luckily, sleep experts say that adults don't need to make up lost sleep hour for hour—it's the dreaming sleep that counts, and that's the kind a tired parent will slip into most easily when the opportunity finally presents itself. Don't feel guilty about doing what's necessary to take care of yourself and get the sleep you need.

If you are nursing, you can pump before you go to sleep and let your partner handle the next feeding, just to get 2 more hours in a row of sleep.

Some parents find their bodies will adapt to this lack of sleep. Others find they just become accustomed to functioning with less energy. According to one study, a marked decrease in energy occurs about two weeks post-partum. Don't over-do it when you first come home with your baby. Your really will need your energy a few weeks later.

The bottom line is this: there's only one person who's going to take care of you—and that's you. You must find ways to deal with fatigue, you must make time just for yourself, and you must learn ways to handle the stress caused by a wakeful baby, newborn or otherwise.

Coping with Fatigue

- Cut your expectations of yourself by at least half. The immaculate home, the gourmet meals, the beautifully organized schedule you've prided yourself on aren't as important right now as taking care of your baby and yourself. Use paper plates and take-out meals for a few weeks—and don't even think about feeling guilty about it. A great deal of exhaustion comes from feeling that there's a right and necessary way to get things done.

- Put a sign on the front door that says "Baby Sleeping...and Mommy, Too," so you won't be disturbed. An old "Do Not Disturb" sign from a hotel can do the trick, too.

- Take the phone off the hook or unplug it!

- Use a telephone answering machine or voice mail. In your recorded message, give the details about your newborn's statistics and progress, say you're resting now, and suggest a time to call that would be more convenient.

- Don't feel you have to entertain all visitors on their schedule. Let them know you have just a half hour to share. If you're uncomfortable about this approach, claim it's doctor's orders.

- Don't feel guilty for wanting your baby to sleep so you can have time to yourself. It's a normal feeling.

- Put the baby in a room other than yours if you are a light sleeper, disturbed by the baby's movements or sounds. When your baby needs you, you'll know it.

- Sleep when your baby sleeps. Don't exhaust yourself by working whenever your baby is sleeping. Match the baby's catnaps with naps of your own, even sitting up, if necessary. Naps restore energy better than any stimulant.

- To refresh yourself when you only have five minutes, visualize something restful like a sunset you've enjoyed. Put your feet up, close your eyes and put your head back.

> I have a quote hanging on my refrigerator door: "Hang Tight! Mothers are doing the most important job in the universe!"
>
> Pam Pierre, Waco, TX

- If you're really in need of sleep, try to nap when the baby naps even when there's an older child on hand. Set up a safe situation such as corralling your child on the couch with you spread lengthwise and play your child's favorite video or DVD.

- Remember that it's okay to get household help. It can be a good investment in you. A temporary housekeeper can be more valuable than a baby nurse.

- Share night feeding with your partner or anyone else available if you can. Even if you're breast-feeding, you can express milk for an occasional bottle. (Remember, too, that a baby who can take a bottle can be left with a sitter for longer periods of time.)

- Give each other a "night off" rather than splitting or sharing a night.

- Take turns playing weekend catch-up, either splitting Saturday and Sunday or alternating weekends, depending on your schedule. The parent "on duty" does whatever is necessary to let the other spouse sleep in.

- Avoid consuming caffeine (at least in quantity), so it doesn't kick in on you when you do have a chance to catnap or sleep.

- Make night feedings more pleasant for yourself. Prepare a thermos with a hot drink for yourself before you go back to bed. When you get up to feed your baby, you'll have something, too. Play tapes, records or listen to the radio. Use a headset so the noise will not bother others.

- Be flexible enough to live with bed-switching when necessary to catch up on sleep. It's not a sign of a deteriorating marriage. Musical beds can be a good, temporary survival tactic.

- Try to live a "timeless" life. Don't upset yourself by looking at the clock every time you're awakened at night. You have to get up anyway; don't make it worse by keeping count of the lost hours of sleep.

- And remind yourself that you're not alone. Try to feel a "spiritual communion" with the millions of other parents doing exactly what you're doing in the middle of the night.

- Keep your sense of humor and learn to make jokes about your lack of sleep and your inconsiderate new family member. A little laughter can reduce stress and recharge your emotional batteries.

Night Work Shift?
Daytime Sleep Tips

Parents who work a night shift and must sleep during daylight hours when kids are awake should keep these tips in mind:

- Wear earplugs when sleeping. Even wearing one cuts down noise yet still allows you to hear an alarm clock.

- Unplug the phone in the bedroom.

- Paint your bedroom a dark color to make it more conducive to sleep.

- Use room-darkening window shades.

- Use "white" noise in the bedroom, such as an inexpensive fan on a night table directed away from the bed.

Coping with Illness—Yours

Becoming sick yourself makes you feel vulnerable, but we all have to deal with this at times so don't be too hard on yourself. Guilt has yet to cure a flu or virus.

- Get help if you can. Even mothers and mothers-in-law may come through for you. Having a sitter is okay, even if you're not deathly ill.

- Take the kids to bed with you and let your bed become the playpen.

- Resorting to television, DVDs and videos as a babysitter is a common coping mechanism.

Private Time

- Realize that you must get away. An hour will help a little; a day would be better. If you can arrange it, a weekend away with your spouse, with a reliable person in charge at home, can work wonders. If you feel guilty about spending the money, think of is as a necessity, not a luxury.

- Don't be afraid to ask for help. Friends, neighbors, or relatives may not be able or willing to take the baby for long, but even an hour alone can give you a lift and a needed rest.

> My quiet time is my bath time, after I've nursed the baby and put my 3-year-old to bed. I take a book into the bathroom for a long bath, even locking the door. It's great.
>
> Kathy Glasgow, Danville, IA

- Devote some time to yourself every day. You'll feel better—still tired, but better—if you're dressed, with hair combed and makeup on. Don't forget nice extra touches like cologne.

- Force yourself to get out of the house on a regular basis, even if it's only to walk the baby outdoors or in a shopping mall.

- Begin to build some exercise into your routine after a few weeks with a new baby. It will help you relax and sleep better when you do sleep.

- Do something unrelated to baby care and housework: go to the library once a week, take a course, sign up for a volunteer job. You may think you're too tired, but the change of pace will refresh you and give you a new perspective on life.

Crying and You

When your baby cries, your blood pressure goes up, your breathing speeds up, and your palms sweat. In addition to these purely physical reactions, you have to deal with mental conflict—how to handle this incessant crying?—and, ultimately, the psychological problems of guilt at your "failure" as a parent, and your anger and hostility toward your baby. When you've done everything you can and the baby is still crying, a seemingly endless cycle begins: fussy baby, tired parent, family tension, more fussiness.

- Take deep breaths to relieve tension.

- Face the fact that you are really angry with this baby who will not let you rest. Write out your anger, talk about it with your spouse and/or a good friend. Discuss it with others in a parenting group.

- In words but not actions, tell your baby how angry you are. If you do it in your sweetest, softest voice, you'll feel better and the baby may be calmed by the sound of your voice.

- Admit to yourself that you're disappointed in your child. Other parents have easy, lovable babies, and it seems unfair that your infant doesn't measure up to your expectations.

- Listen to the advice well-meaning friends and relatives are almost certainly giving you—some of it may be worthwhile—but don't feel you have to try everything they suggest.

- And don't listen to criticism! Say you're working with your doctor on the baby's problem, if you must say something, and that you are optimistic about finding a solution soon.

- Finally, give yourself permission to cry, too. Sometimes that's the best remedy of all.

Seeking Professional Help

Don't hesitate to get professional help when you feel you're nearing the end of your rope. Seeking help is a sign of intelligence and strength, not of weakness.

Parents Anonymous is a national organization of self-help groups for parents who are afraid they may ultimately abuse their children. Write to them at 675 West Foothills Blvd #220, Claremont, CA 91711. Call 909-621-6184 or check their website (www.parentsanonymous.org) for information about a group near you.

Prevent Child Abuse (PCA) **America** is a national volunteer-based organization dedicated to stopping child abuse before it starts. For a free information packet, including tips on parenting, write Prevent Child Abuse, 200 S. Michigan, Suite 1700, Chicago, IL 60604. Or you can call 312-663-3520. Their web address is: www. preventchildabuse.org.

Chapter 8

— Naptime —
How Long Will It Last?

Children nap because, yes, they do require extra sleep to function. We all know that a tired child loses control easily. And an overly tired child can have a very hard time falling asleep and sleeping soundly. Sometimes an overtired child can display "hyper" behavior when exhausted instead of falling right to sleep as we expect.

You probably need that naptime, too. As one parent said, "naps are the glue that holds a mother together."

Really Napping

Most infants take their morning nap about two hours after they wake up. When your child is between 1 and 2 years old, you can expect a consolidation of the morning and afternoon naps. By age 2, most children are taking just one nap a day, usually after lunch. This transition requires schedule flexibility on your part for a while—most specifically when you work out your lunchtime. Between the age of 3 and 4 most kids give up naps, though many do it earlier than this.

Some children go willingly to bed for naps; others resist. Often the unwillingness to nap is simply normal resistance to an established routine. A resting routine during the day is a good idea for these children—and their parents.

Setting the Stage

- Place your baby down in the same location as for nighttime to keep the association with sleep.

- Clear the crib of toys and other fun distractions.

- Condense your bedtime routine if it's too lengthy for naptime, but follow a few regular procedures, such as reading a story, tucking the child in comfortably, and giving a "good nap" kiss.

- Play a white noise tape, such as a recording of your vacuum cleaner, just as you would at bedtime.

- Separate two children who share a room if you expect either to sleep.

- A bed tent can be an ideal napping environment.

- Let a child who's resisting a nap lie with you on your bed for a few minutes until the child or both of you fall asleep.

- Lie down with your child on a bed with an electric blanket and turn it on while you're snuggling. It will make sleep come more easily.

- Don't tiptoe around or avoid flushing toilets when your child is napping. A child should be able to sleep through the normal noises of household activity.

And What Do Moms Do During Naptime?

First, I leap about, cheering. Then I clean one room and sit there.

A. Hurst, Ottawa, Ont.

I read, study, write letters, occasionally nap myself—but never housework. My husband shares that, so I never feel a need to do anything during naptime. We all work together in the evening. That one or two hours every afternoon keeps me sane.

Phoebe Resnick, Broomall, PA

I swing into action and clean the bathrooms or any part of the house that is hard to clean with the children around. My time to relax is at night when the children are in bed, though I still find myself doing "just one more thing."

Corinne Powell, Dyer, IN

NAP! (Providing both kids nap at the same time, the doorbell doesn't ring, the Avon lady doesn't come, the washer doesn't throw itself off balance, the dryer buzzer doesn't go off, the dishwasher doesn't flood the kitchen, I don't break my neck falling over toys on the way to the bedroom, the boss isn't coming to dinner, and a telephone solicitor doesn't call trying to waterproof the basement I don't have.)

Jan Schmitz, St. Louis, MO

"What? Wake a Sleeping Child?"

- Wake your child after about two hours of afternoon napping so your child will be able to sleep at bedtime. Or time the nap so your child will wake up at least four hours before bedtime.

- Don't scold a child who wakes up cross and irritable. Ignore the grouchiness, offer a snack, and go about your business until the child comes around. Some children experience more disorientation upon waking than others.

- Wake your child by making noises around the room or just by straightening up, rather than approaching your child directly.

- Read to wake your child up. It's a good way to make a smooth transition to a wakeful state for one who usually wakes up angry.

When Naps End

- Be prepared to abandon naps when they interfere with a child's sleep at night.

- Prepare to shift mealtimes (a later lunch, perhaps, and earlier dinner). Transitions usually call for changes in schedules.

- Wean a young child off a pacifier, bottle, or breast during this transition. Your child won't need any of those at naptime anymore and that may be a way to begin the process.

- Don't go on car rides at inappropriate times when your child might fall asleep, if you don't want to throw off whatever is left of the schedule. Or try the reverse. When trying to get your child onto an after lunch nap schedule, take a drive after lunch for a few days in a row to get your child used to falling asleep at that time. It should be easier to have naps reinstituted at home at the same time each day.

- Plan for about 3 weeks of adjustment to no naps and expect some early evening temper tantrums. Keep expectations low at this time.

> I'm usually wiped out when naptime for my 2-year-old twins rolls around. I get myself a pillow and a blanket and camp out on the floor (guarding the door so they can't get out). I leave the crib side down so they can get a toy if they want one, give each a few books—then I crash! I have my standard line: "We're all resting now, we have our books. Let Mom sleep." If I'm not tired, I bring in a book to read or checkbook to balance, etc. I get a lot accomplished and it sure beats hassling with them about going to bed.
>
> Sue Schuessler, Barrington, IL

Just Resting

Often by age 3, and almost always by age 5, children simply don't need naps anymore. There is no way you can force a wide-awake child to sleep. Still, the child needs a change of pace, and you probably need a little respite, too. Quiet time, rest time, or whatever you want to call it can save you both from an unpleasant late afternoon and evening. Establish this as a routine with limitations and benefits of it's own.

- Go along with a child who tries to please you by pretending to be asleep. Occasionally your child may actually doze off.

- Set a gate across your child's bedroom door as a reminder to stay in that room during "naptime."

- Insist that the resting child stay in one place for the whole rest period.

- Bring out special toys or a toy that is only available in your child's room and during "naptime."

- Be sure to call your child to indicate the end of the rest period. If you don't do this consistently, your child may get into the habit of calling you frequently to ask if the time is up yet.

- Set a timer or put on a stack of records or a tape/CD to last through the hour or so of rest time. Or show your child where the hands on the clock will be when he or she may get up.

The side benefit of the end of naptime is that your child will now, in all probability, be going to bed earlier and giving you more private time in the evening.

Great Places to Nap or Rest

- Anyone else's bed.

- A sleeping bag on a bed or a couch, or on the floor in any room.

- A big appliance box suitably padded with blankets and pillows.

- Under a desk, table, card table, or other piece of furniture— best if covered with a sheet or blanket, for privacy!

- A tent in the backyard near the house, if neighbor children won't be around.

Chapter 9

What Are Reasonable Bedtime Routines for My Older Child?

In some families, "going to sleep," at any time of the day or night, is a struggle for control, from a child's infancy right through the school years. In other families, the struggle doesn't begin in earnest until a child is about 2 and is anxious to assert independence. Some children simply aren't sleepy when their parents think they should be; others fight sleep as if it were the enemy.

Learn your child's "tired" signals—rubbing eyes or ears, staring off into space, thumb-sucking, etc.—so you can start bedtime before over-tiredness sets in.

One thing that helps in almost every case is a bedtime routine appropriate to the child's age and the circumstances of your family life. They help active toddlers shift down into a calmer, or more conducive bedtime setting. Don't worry that you'll be setting up a program you'll have to follow for the next ten years; any ritual will change and evolve as your child grows, and you'll probably find that the fifteen or twenty minutes you spend with your child at bedtime can be a really pleasant experience.

Or maybe your child really isn't all that tired. Might you be letting the child sleep too late in the morning? Maybe you need to consider advancing your child's morning wake-up time. Do so gradually, by ten-minute increments. (Use the same gradual change if you want to move bedtime earlier as naps are phased out.)

Probably the best way to handle continuous conflict is to try to avoid making a big issue of bedtime—another piece of advice that's easier said than done. It's also important never to make going to bed a punishment.

You Can't Control Your Child's Going to Sleep. You Can Only Control Your Child's Bedtime.
(most of the time)

As your child gets older, bedtime routines can be more fun (because of language ability) and harder to accomplish (who wants such a terrific day to end?).

Most parents find that it doesn't pay to rush the bedtime routine. Better to start it earlier if that fits your schedule.

Be sure you have everything your need—dolls, stuffed animals, books, security blanket—in the bed before you leave the room. In fact, encourage the company of a favorite soft toy or security blanket. These can be wonderful substitutes for a parent and help in the transition to independence from parental attachment.

Another good routine is to let your child say goodnight to all the dolls and toys. That way your child will be the last one in the room to whom you say goodnight.

Some parents who have stayed beside their children until they have fallen asleep may have to change that—either dramatically by calling an end to that routine, or gradually ending it over a period of a few weeks. This can be done by first sitting beside the bed, then no longer stroking the child, then moving the chair a few feet away from the bed. Next the chair should be near the door and finally outside the bedroom!

Our daughter has never been on a schedule. When she turned 1, I simply let her stay up until she got tired (anywhere from 9:30—11 p.m.). A few minutes of rocking and she's sound asleep. I think not forcing a schedule on her makes her a happier, contented baby.

Sue Malley, Kalamazoo, MI

Daddy's arm is my son's security blanket since he sleeps with us and likes to curl up around it or have it around him at sleep time. It has lasted three years, but we hope to get him into his own bed soon.

Judy Jung, Austin, TX

Bedtime Routines for Toddlers

Try to put your toddler to bed at the same time every night. Children of this age love their bedtime routines and often try to make them last as long as possible. And this is the age when most children start insisting that nothing in the routine can be changed. After all, routines make life safe and predictable. They also have the important function of marking the end of the day's events and relationships. That final drink of water is more than a drink. It is a final gift from a parent that affirms love and attention.

Take turns going through the bedtime routine with your partner so your child won't come to insist that the same parent do the honors every night.

In the toddler years when everything meets with resistance, give positive choices whenever possible. "Do you want to wear the red or blue pajamas?" Or "Which animal gets to sleep with you tonight?"

- Warn your child that bedtime is approaching. Ten minutes' advance notice is usually enough. Set a timer or watch alarm to announce it. Think of it as the PJ alarm—as well as the start of your bedtime routine.

- Have "quiet time" prior to bedtime so a child isn't over stimulated. A keyed-up child is not only harder to get to sleep, but also is more likely to wake during the night. Young children rarely possess the ability to calm themselves down. Rocking a toddler can be a wonderful way to end the day.

- Incorporate tooth brushing, washing or bathing, and putting pajamas on into the bedtime routine.

- Get into the habit of saying an evening prayer, if you like.

- Don't use lengthy bedtime routines to compensate for not having seen your child all day of you're a working parent. Trying to pack too many good things into a short period can over stimulate your child.

- Pick a book to read, and make it one that you like, too. It will probably be requested often. Don't read a word until your child is in pajamas and/or under the covers.

- Read poetry for a change. The rhythm has a relaxing effect.

- Sing softly to your child.

- Talk about what you'll do tomorrow, even if it's only what you'll have for breakfast. Say that the sooner the child falls asleep, the sooner tomorrow will come.

- Provide your child with a decorative, active clock (like a Mickey Mouse clock with moving hands or a winking eye) to watch. This helps the child learn about telling time while getting to sleep with this variation on "counting sheep."

- Turn on a cassette/CD/record of soft, soothing music.

- Play a radio, with an automatic shut-off timing feature, as a routine at bedtime. It may also serve to keep a child in bed and lessen the loneliness of bedtime.

- Or set a music box to play.

- Make a big deal out of turning off the bedroom light, or letting your child do it.

- Or make a ritual of "blowing out" the bedroom light.

- Kiss your child's palm, close the fingers around the kiss and tell your child to save it until the morning when it can be "given back."

- Help your child get ready for sleep by snuggling in his or her bed, or in yours, if the child is still in a crib.

- Let your last act be tucking in your child tightly for a good, snug feeling of security.

> An hour before bedtime we turn our "stars" (glow-in-the-dark stickers put up on the ceiling) on by turning on the room light. I've also heard there is a luminous paint and stencil kit that does this too. When she's ready and yawning we go in, turn off the light and watch the stars.
>
> Bonnie Madsen, Brooklyn Center, MN

Moving Up to the Big Bed

Most children are thrilled to graduate to an adult bed, and the transition usually goes smoothly. If the move is to make a crib ready for a soon-to-be-born sibling, make the new bed move at least two months in advance of the event, or consider buying or borrowing a second crib.

You should be able to find one or more books that address this issue. Reading about a child's similar experience always helps children with changes.

- Keep bedtime rituals as consistent as possible.

- Give your child a familiar toy to take to bed, even a too-small, old blanket allows familiar items to be at hand.

- Ease the transition by removing one side of the crib to make it seem like a real bed.

- Let the child sleep on a pillow in the crib before the move. This will help your child learn to center his or her body in a bed.

- Buying a new bed? Bring your child with you and take your child's wishes into consideration.

- Keep the new bed in the same position as the old crib, if possible.

- Push one side of the bed up against the wall, and put the old crib mattress on the floor on the other side, in case of a fall.

- Or set the mattress and box spring on the floor the first week or so. If your child rolls off, the floor is only a few inches away.

- Let your child help pick out the linens for the big bed, especially if he or she is a bit reluctant to make the move. Bed "tents" are another way to encourage a move.

- Turn favorite crib sheets into pillowcases for the look and feel of something familiar.

- If you have the room, keep the bed and the crib in the same room and let your child choose where to sleep for a few weeks.

- Make a "valley" for the child to sleep in by putting a rolled blanket on either side of—but under—the center of the mattress.

- Let your child use the big bed first as a place to nap. A new nap place is exciting) while continuing to use the crib at night for security.

- Take a photo of your child going to sleep in the big bed to make that evening a special event.

- Put off the move for a few weeks if the child really protests the dismantling of the crib.

We have a solid routine that both parents have memorized. Each child is given time to talk, relax and snuggle with us. If we push or rush it never pays. They need our time and patience.

Jodi Junge, Bryn Athyn, PA

Lie down with them. Read stories and stay with them until they fall asleep. This ruins your free time in the evenings for years, but so far it's worth it!

Pat Plack, Brimfield, IL

"I Want A Glass of Water" Syndrome

Children often test your limits by stretching bedtime rituals. Rational explanations will not be as effective as simple, consistent rules for bedtime.

- Expect some calls (for a drink, if nothing else) after your child has been kissed for the last time, though try to remember to ask your child if there is anything needed before you leave the room. Return or not, as you wish, but be reasonably consistent from night to night. Or keep a capped water bottle or plastic glass by the bedside. (Keep in mind that too many liquids can cause wakefulness and will be a real deterrent to conquering bed-wetting later, when toilet training begins.)

- Any trip out of bed should be prompt and with as little attention as possible.

Refusing to Stay in Bed

- Give steps and consequences so your child will know what to expect, such as no story the next night.

- Use a gate or close the child's bedroom door, letting your child know the door will stay open if he or she stays in bed.

- Provide your child with 3 "pass tickets" (or any number of your choosing) to surrender when coming out the bedroom. It helps limit trips.

- Listen outside the door so you can pop in quickly if you hear your child getting out of bed.

- Lead a child back to bed gently but without a word! Be matter-of-fact, like a robot. Don't react—and don't get discouraged. Refusing to stay in bed may go on for a long time but it will not go on forever.

- Tell your child to listen quietly for the sounds made by whoever is still awake. Kids can hear you washing dishes, watching TV, brushing your teeth, etc. This gives a feeling of security by staying in touch with you even though you're not there.

- Be firm. Say, "Goodnight. And I mean it!"

- Or go to sleep yourself, turn off lights, and eliminate your child's reason for wanting to stay up.

- Be lavish with praise in the morning after your child has stayed in bed. Praise again during the next night's bedtime routine.

- If fear of the dark is part of this problem, see pg 131 for additional ideas.

Just Can't Relax

Put perfume (or some scented powder) on your child's hand and ask your child to take long, deep breaths until the smell is gone. That's a good way to get a child in bed and to combine concentration, relaxation and deep breathing.

Routines for Preschoolers

Bedtime problems may begin to develop with preschoolers who have previously gone to bed willingly. If things are going well in other areas, don't worry. Set your own limits about how much stalling you'll tolerate. Preschoolers' lives are exciting, and unwinding at night may take some time.

Routines now will probably be elaborate and drawn out. You may have to worry about such things as tucking in the blanket just the right way and being sure that every toy in the room has been kissed goodnight. And your child may insist that toys and clothing be arranged just right. Bedtime rituals seem to change just as you're getting used to them. That's part of their changing, so stay flexible.

Many of the previously listed tips should work for you as well as some of these listed for the older child.

- Give longer notice about bedtime than you did when the child was younger. Now a child is probably old enough so you can show where the hands of the clock will be when it's time for bed.

- Put your child to bed—sending your child to bed seldom works. You do have to continue to set aside time from chores or TV for some or all of your child's bedtime routine.

- Give an older child a snack of protein and carbohydrates before bedtime to encourage sounder sleep. Oatmeal is a good example of this combination. Milk supplies the protein, and the oats supply the carbohydrates.

- Read or tell a story regularly. You may be asked for the same one every night, but some children are ready now for more variety. Older preschoolers often like to hear a chapter of a long book every night.

- Make changes in routines gradually. Cuddle in your child's bed instead of in yours; switch from a lullaby to a record/tape/CD of a favorite song.

- Tape yourself reading or singing one night. Use the tape the next night. Then have it available for your sitter at bedtime.

At 2, my second son would NOT stay in bed. I decided he needed more time with me and less sleep so I extended his bedtime to 9:30-10 p.m. He often fell asleep on the floor! At 4 now, he goes to his bed at 8:30 p.m. but often reads and "plays" until 10 p.m. When he wakes up he is cheerful and alert. We've had to adapt to his lower-than-average need for sleep.

A. Hoffer, McLean, VA

We open up our hide-a-bed in the family room and our 2-year-old falls peacefully asleep between us while we watch TV at night. Then I put her to bed.

Barbara Yanez, Martinez, CA

- Review the day's events and talk about tomorrow, even if it's only what you think the weather will be.

- Use the last few minutes before lights out every night to tell your child one good thing about himself or herself. It will build self-esteem and should inspire sweet dreams as well.

- Turn off the lights and listen together for sounds of the night while you snuggle.

- Use the reward technique for this age child—be it stars on a chart or the promise of something special—if bedtime conditions have been met for a full week.

- Let your child know what you'll be doing while he or she is going to sleep, but don't make it sound like too much fun.

- Distinguish between "bedtime" and "sleep time." Let your child play or read alone in bed for a few minutes if he or she goes to bed early enough.

Good Bedtime Reading

Bedtime reading helps set the stage both through listening to the calming voice of a reader and also through sharing the bedtime routine. Some authors poke fun at the bedtime ritual; others celebrate it. All recognize the importance of the day's closing moments.

"Goodnight Moon" by Margaret Wise Brown (HarperCollins) has become the classic bedtime story. This book lovingly names and says good night to each of the objects in a young bunny's bedroom, confirming that everything is as it should be and that they will still be there in the morning.

There are always a variety of 'go-to-sleep' titles available from your library or bookstore. There are many old favorites as well as new ones to choose from.

To Sleep, Perhaps to Dream

After Jason (3-1/2) has bathed and been read to, we say goodnight and start our "five minute checks." Every five minutes one of us goes in and says, "How are you? Goodnight. See you in five minutes." He's happy and bedtime has become sane and almost pleasant at our house.

Christina Klecka, Budd Lake, NJ

Our 4-year-old gave up naps at 2 and still resists bedtime. Ritual became the key word. ALWAYS: (1) bathroom, (2) brush teeth, (3) share a story, (4) goodnight! Now that she is older, we let her play a radio quietly to lull her to sleep.

Judy Deuel, West Bloomfield, MI

One of our best routines is to let our daughter listen to one cassette tape. By the second side, she is usually asleep.

The Lipmans, A. Windham, ME

I award a star to each child for every night of no-hassle bedtime. Each star is worth a quarter and they select a prize at the store on Saturday, spending only what they have earned.

Myra Weaver, Hollywood, FL

At bedtime a story or two (or three or four) works well. Also we resort to threats and bribery on occasion.

Pam Torborg, Armonk, NY

How Do I Handle Fears and Bad Dreams?

From about 18 months on, children develop fears of various kinds. Don't make light of any fear, however ridiculous it may seem to you. Never ignore fears or overreact to them. Some fears are almost impossible to put into words, as is the case of various sensations felt as a child drifts off to sleep—for example, the convulsive jerk the body sometimes makes. Whatever your child's fear, confront it, explain it as best you can, support your child as that child confronts the fear, and do what you can to alleviate it.

Avoid scary bedtime stories, and monitor television programs carefully if your child is prone to bad dreams. Feel free to encourage bedtime companions such as security blankets, dolls, and stuffed animals. Consider yourself lucky if your child has an imaginary playmate to go to bed with at night. Don't discourage rituals the child may devise to feel safe.

Calming fears usually requires your presence. If necessary, sit on the bed, in a chair, whatever, just so your child doesn't feel alone. Maybe you have a pet which can serve this function for you. Deep breathing relaxation exercises can help your child relax in many situations. A back rub can help, too.

Fear of Separation

For a child who is afraid you'll leave the house after being put to bed, leave something of yourself (shoes, car keys, etc.) in the child's bedroom for reassurance. For a child under the age of 1 who doesn't really understand that a parent exists when out of his or her sight:

- Give your baby a little "practice" by playing peek-a-boo, hiding your face, and showing your baby that you always "come back".

- Or hide behind a door, popping out after a few seconds.

- Leave the baby's door open at night so he or she can hear your voice and know that you're not far away.

When a Sitter Sits in for You

Don't leave your baby with an unfamiliar sitter when your baby is sleeping. It's unsettling, if not downright frightening, to wake up to a stranger. Babies know who is familiar and who is not, starting at around 5 months. Let a child old enough to understand, know that you will be going out while he or she is asleep, but you will be there in the morning.

- Don't sneak out on an awake child. Better to face the tears—which usually end once you are out the door.

- Engage your sitter and child in a fun activity before you exit.

- Cultivate one or two sitters who your baby will know—as well as good relationships with your parents and your in-laws.

- Advise your sitter not to play audio equipment too loud (or wear headsets) so as not to be able to hear a crying baby.

- Familiarize your sitter with your child's bedtime routine. If your child normally has a nighttime snack, favorite toy, security blanket or bedtime book, be sure to let the sitter know in advance.

- Know that this child who is devastated by the fact that you are leaving (if only temporarily) will not blink an eye at your departure a few years from now.

Fear of the Dark

Find out what your child imagines is happening in the dark. Offer verbal reassurances about the dark but there are lots of practical, little things you can do too.

- Consider putting an aquarium in a fearful child's room. The light and movement may help lull your child to sleep.

- Leave on a night-light in your child's room, or leave the door open and the hall light on. If you wish, attach your night light to an automatic timer that will turn it off after your child has fallen asleep, say at midnight.

- Purchase star stickers that glow in the dark to put on the child's ceiling. Sing "Twinkle, Twinkle, Little Star" in bed together. Ask your child to watch for the shooting or falling star. Chances are your child will fall asleep before seeing one.

- Give a child of 3 or so a flashlight to shine when fear strikes. (If it is the type that unscrews, tape both ends tightly, or you'll find it in pieces in the morning.)

- Learn a poem or song a child can use for self-comfort when scared of the dark.

- Install a dimmer switch that can be lowered by tiny bits every night.

- Kiss your child goodnight and close with the words, "We love you and will protect you at all times."

- Take your child out at night to show the magic of darkness. Lie on a blanket in your yard on a warm night, watching for fireflies, looking at the stars, and listening to night sounds.

Our son has a fit if his light is turned off. We argued over this for a while and then I decided—"Where is it written you must sleep with the light off?" For his comfort and peace of mind, I leave it on.

Susan Lipke, Harrietta, MI

Fear of a Storm

- Play favorite tapes or records loud enough to block or offset sounds of heavy weather.

- Sit with your child in bed until the major part of the storm passes.

- Have your child "boom!" back at the sound of thunder.

My 4-year-old is scared of storms so we just tell her it's the angels in heaven bowling and taking pictures.

Mrs. Rick Johns, Crete, NE

Fear of Shadows

- Move the child's bed to a "safe" place in the room.

- Get an opaque window shade.

- Find the source of the shadow in the room and point it out in the daytime, or with the lights on.

- Make shadows interesting rather than scary by practicing finger shadow play with your child. (You remember: a closed fist with index and middle fingers raised makes a bunny.)

- Or play, "silhouettes" by focusing a shadow on a big piece of paper taped to the wall and filling it in with a black marker.

- Teach your child the old favorite from *The King and I*, "I'll Whistle a Happy Tune."

- Show a child, during playtime on a sunny day, that he or she casts a shadow, too.

Fear of Monsters and Other Scary Creatures

- Reduce or eliminate viewing of violent TV and cartoon programs.

- Look under the bed with the child, or in the closet, or out the window—where ever monsters lurk. Shine a flashlight all around the room to prove it's safe. Leave on the closet light if the "monsters" come from inside the closet.

- Place the mattress and box spring on the floor so there is no space for monsters to hide. This is a reasonable, time-limited solution.

- Create a magic curse to make them disappear.

- Provide a 'Dragon Deterrent' magic potion (a special box filled with potpourri or any thing you creatively concoct).

- Destroy the monster. Bring a big bag into the room to "capture" scary creatures, tie it shut, and take it out to the garbage can. Or spray them away with a spritz of cologne, air freshener, or hair spray. Flushing them down the toilet may also work.

- If there is an older sibling who will share a room for a few weeks, let that child move in if that will allay any fears.

> To keep the "lions" away at night, we have her inflatable elephant and teddy bear positioned on her bed to stand guard.
>
> C.R. Hillard, Cadillac, MI
>
> We put up a sign on the door saying, STOP, MONSTERS NOT ALLOWED. It helped for a while.
>
> Jane Berkowicz, Hartsdale, NY

Fear of Death

A death in the family can precipitate nightmares.

- Be very careful not to equate death with sleep, or your child may be afraid of going to sleep and never waking up. When people die, they do not go to sleep.

- Explain death as best you can, in religious terms if you wish. If someone in or close to your family dies, let your child grieve with you. Be honest with your child and give your child a chance to discuss any fears.

- Be sure your child understands thoroughly that the death was in no way caused by anything done or thought. Wishing a person dead doesn't make it so. It is only a common expression of anger.

- Reassure your child that everyone in your home is well. Talk about how we can live a long life by eating correctly, using safety belts and seeing the doctor regularly. This helps give children a feeling of control over their body.

Bad Dreams or Nightmares

Bad dreams begin to occur around the end of a child's second year. They seem to follow a pattern. The victim—your child—is confronted by a life-threatening creature or situation. These dreams seem very real because the boundaries between fantasy and reality are blurred at this age. As an adult, you might compare a child's bad dream to one of your own—the one in which you're being chased but can't run.

Help your child understand that dreams are a form of make-believe. The dream isn't real but the feelings they produce are, which is why we can't make light of them.

A dream often dramatizes a conflict in a child's life, be it divorce, the child's own aggressiveness, or guilt based on some event. They also evolve as more demands for autonomy and maturity are placed on a child. Dreams are outlets for feelings.

- Respond to a bad dream as you would to a fright in the daytime. Don't make light of the fear, but don't overreact, either. Liken it to a story one makes up when asleep.

- Be sure your child is really awake so the dream won't continue. Wipe your child's face with a warm, damp washcloth, or make a trip to the bathroom to use the toilet.

- Lie in bed with and snuggle your child until sleep returns.

- Hug and reassure the child but don't ask to hear about the dream unless your child wants to talk about it. Describing the details of the dream may upset your child again.

- Have your child shake his or her head—hard—to shake out all the bad dreams.

- Tell your child to "change the channel" in his or her head.

- Leave the light on in your child's room if that's what is needed for reassurance. A child doesn't understand "it's only a dream."

- Let your child camp out in a sleeping bag on the floor next to your bed if awoken by nightmares.

- Talk a little about the dream the next day if your child remembers it and wants to discuss it. Tell your child that you have bad dreams sometimes, too—everyone does—and tell him or her what you do when you have one.

- Ask your child to draw a picture of the frightening dream the day after. Then talk about how the monster could be defeated or a bad situation could be changed. This helps a child learn how to "control" a repeating nightmare.

> When my daughter has a bad dream, I usually rock her and try to get her to tell me about it. When she is ready to go back to bed, I turn her pillow over because the bad dream is on that side. This little thing seems to help her get back to sleep more easily.
>
> Susan Cooper, Franklin, MA

Preventing Bad Dreams

- Make a Dream Jar and decorate it appropriately. With your child, think of every lovely dream one could have. Write each one on a slip of paper and take one out of the jar every night at bedtime.

- Spray a bit of cologne on your child's pillow to induce "sweet dreams."

- Hang a picture of a "guardian angel" or a Native American dream catcher near your child's bed for security. These can 'catch' the bad dreams so you are only left with the good ones. Or maybe a picture of Grandma and Grandpa who will watch over their grandchild.

- Create a soft toy with different colored buttons sewn on it. Let a child press one of the buttons to select a dream or change a bad one.

- Keep a wind-up toy radio or music box next to the bed for a child to use if awoken by a bad dream.

- Give your child a pleasant image to concentrate on while falling asleep—a white bunny hopping through the snow, for example.

- Let your child go to bed in Super Hero pajamas for a feeling of extra security.

- Read books with your child that help put scary thoughts into words and pictures to help put bad dreams "to bed." Some favorites are: "My Mama Says There Aren't Any Zombies, Ghosts or Vampires" by Judith Viorst (Atheneum); "There's a Nightmare in My Closet" by Mercer Mayer (Dial); and "Where the Wild Things Are" by Maurice Sendak (HarperCollins).

We try to replace bad thoughts with good ones, and name all the things that make us happy. We learned this from "The Sound of Music."

Carol Taylor, Birmingham, AL

Watching TV with the kids and watching their reactions helps me to deal with their fears when they occur.

Pat Omans, Berkeley, MI

Night or Sleep Terrors

About 5% of children from age 4 or 5 to about 6 or 8 have night terrors, which are different from nightmares. Night terrors occur during the deepest sleep, about 1 to 4 hours after bedtime, not during the dreaming state. The child sits up in bed, screaming with terror, thrashing about, often with eyes wide open, but not really awake. An episode can last 10 to 30 minutes. Heart and respiration rates are high.

A child who has had a night terror seems calm when finally awake while a child with a bad dream will more likely awaken crying or frightened. A night terror is NOT a bad dream or a psychotic attack. It is an episode of intense terror during sleep. Night terrors often are forgotten the next day, and there's little you can do about them when they occur except wait for them to subside. Most children won't be aware that they've had a night terror, whereas with a bad dream the child may want to talk about the dream. It appears boys are more likely to have night terrors than girls, though researchers don't know why.

- Don't try to wake a child in the grip of a night terror. Your child may slip back into deep sleep within a few minutes.

- Don't restrain your child during an episode but be sure your child is protected from injury.

- Reassure your child with hugging and holding.

- If the child wakes up, make a trip to the bathroom. Familiar sounds and actions may have a calming effect.

- If night terrors are frequent, see your doctor. Your child may need professional help.

Sleepwalking

Doctors aren't sure why kids sleepwalk but they know it affects more boys than girls and tends to run in families. A child who walks or talks while sleeping does so during the deepest stage of sleep and is not "acting out" a dream. The cause may be immaturity of the nervous system, which interferes with a smooth passage through the various sleep cycles. It's estimated that about 15% of children have one or more episodes of sleepwalking, and most talk in their sleep, usually incoherently. This child may just sit up in bed, with eyes wide open, and move around a bit and perhaps talk a little, or he or she may get out of bed to walk around and leave the room or even the house. Many episodes occur only once a month. If they are nightly or your sleepwalker exits the house, it may be time to consult with your doctor.

While a sleepwalker appears to be aware of the surroundings, actually this is not the case. Your sleepwalker will have little if any recollection of the night's events the following day. The highest prevalence of sleepwalking (16%) is at ages 11 to 12.

- Guide your child gently back to bed, possibly stopping in the bathroom first. Talk softly and reassuringly.

- Take your choice between two pieces of conflicting advice. Some say never to wake a sleepwalker because doing so will be frightening or cause confusion. Others recommend waking the child to start a sleep cycle afresh.

- Take the same precautions for a sleepwalker that you would for a toddler given to wandering around at night. Put a gate at the child's door, or hang a bell that will wake you up if the door is opened. Be sure windows and doors in the house are locked.

It's not easy to prevent sleepwalking but keeping your child on a regular schedule and getting enough sleep may help. If your child wanders at a regular time, set your alarm 15-30 minutes before this time and gently waken your child. This may 'reset' your child's biological clock.

If a child begins to have fears, nightmares, or severe difficulty in falling asleep and all of these measures don't work after a few weeks, the child should be seen by a pediatrician or family counselor. Something may be disturbing the child in daily life. This kind of sudden onset and persistence is seen in children who have been sexually abused.

Pleasant Dreams

Index

SLEEP
Not the Impossible Dream!

Getting Your Child to Sleep...and Back to Sleep (book) $9.95
 lullaby music with womb/heartbeat sounds plus spoken tips:
  Getting Your Baby to Sleep (60 min)   audio tape $9.95
                                  CD (music only) $10.95

. . . .

"Some of the very best solutions for sleep problems."
                                    - Louise Bates Ames, Gessell Institute

. . . .

Other books for new parents by Vicki Lansky include:

 FEED ME I'M YOURS
 PRACTICAL PARENTING TIPS YRS 1-5
 BEST NEW BABY TIPS
 GAMES BABIES PLAY
 TROUBLE-FREE TRAVEL WITH CHILDREN
 BABYPROOFING BASICS

To order any of the above or to get a free catalog of all her titles
call 1-800-255-3379 or write DearVicki@aol.com
visit www.practicalparenting.com

Practical Parenting, 15245 Minnetonka Blvd, Minnetonka, MN 55345
(952) 912-0036 · fax (952) 912-0105